MW01492120

Orphans No More

Learning to Live Loved

Dudley Hall

KERYGMA VENTURES PRESS
Euless, Texas

To the various men's groups

who helped to clarify the message by listening

and asking insightful questions

as we together seek to abandon our orphan mindset

and live as sons.

Introduction

I have a dear friend and treasured co-worker in Wade Trimmer of Augusta, Georgia. On his own initiative, he compiled a series of my monthly messages and put them in book form, spurring me to get serious about putting this message in print.

Wade wrote,
"Well Glory! This is Dudley. It is good to be back with you this month." For those who have been a subscriber to Dudley Hall's Message of the Month for any length of time, you have, in all probability, inserted the tape or compact disk into your player and repeated with the Dud the above opening statement. This familiar voice and phrase is so welcome because you know that a 'father in the faith' is about to speak into your life again with life-transforming biblical truth.

This short book is an introduction to the most liberating truth ever revealed to mankind. We discover that we can actually know God personally like Jesus the Son does. We are stunned by the reality that we can live engulfed in his unconditional and eternal love... like Jesus the Son.

Orphaned by Adam's sin, we are adopted on the basis of Jesus' sonship. The relationship is made experiential by the presence of the Holy Spirit in us crying, "Abba, Father." No longer defined by our separation from God, we are sons whose passion is to honor our Father.

Spiritual orphans spend their lives longing to belong. Spiritual sons are at home in the Father's house and spend their lives working with him.

It is no accident that reality as defined by God's witness in Scripture is framed in the Father-Son dynamic. "Father" is not just another metaphor like rock or shepherd to help us get a concept of God. Father, Son and Spirit eternally describe God. The amazing hope of the gospel is that we can actually enjoy the life shared by the Father and the Son. We are invited to enjoy the eternal life of knowing God as the Son has revealed him.

This is such a big dynamic it will take eternity for us to discover all the ramifications. I hope this brief collection of messages introduces you to the possibilities available through the gospel. I pray that it will help open your eyes to a fresh way of seeing our plight and our privilege. In a future book I plan to more fully develop the themes that are introduced here. Join me in the adventure of recognizing the symptoms of orphan thinking and displacing that thinking with the truth of being sons of God.

I pray this introduction will whet your appetite to abandon all forms of orphan thinking by trusting the Father's love.

Dudley Hall
October 2011

Table of Contents

1. Living As Sons of God

If the Biblical perspective is trusted, the answer to mankind's nagging question is clearly answered: "What is life really about?" It is about a Father and Son relationship. Trying to make sense of it without this dynamic is futile. Just knowing theoretically about the Father and Son does not satisfy the universal longing of mankind's soul. Man was created to live in conscious fellowship with the Father, and when that relationship is absent, life begins to deteriorate quickly.

Adam, The First Son of God

The Genesis account relates how God created Adam as his first son. Before the rib surgery, Eve was part of Adam and thus a son of God as well, and she continued in that relationship even after the division. Adam and Eve were so conscious of the Father that they were unconcerned about their flesh. They related to the Father of spirits, focusing on the intimacy of fellowship and the meaningfulness of partnership. They didn't worry about provision since the garden trees were laden with fruit for every taste. They didn't fret about protection because they were under the care of the Father and all his mighty angels. They did not strive for position because they were aware that they were the crown of the Father's creation and responsible for its care.

But then they sinned. When they chose to accept the accusa-tion of the Accuser, life changed. The serpent told them that God was holding something back from them and that they could do something to exalt their status even higher. The serpent was attacking their role as sons. Believing that they could subdue the earth without being subdued by the Father, they ate from the forbidden tree of the knowledge of good and evil. Instead of relying on their spiritual connection with the Father they chose to get their information elsewhere. Suddenly they were afraid and hid behind a bush from the very Father who had created and cared for them. They were now more focused on their flesh than on the Father. They were self-conscious rather than being Father-conscious. They introduced the "flesh perspective" to humanity, defining life more in terms of the physical, natural, survival, and self-serving mentality than the satisfying intimacy that character-ized their spiritual communion. This flesh focus became the default mode of perceiving life for all following races of people.

Another way of describing this condition is fatherlessness. When Adam and Eve hid, they demonstrated their alienation from the Father. They saw themselves, for the first time, isolated from relationship with the Father. So we can say that at this point fatherlessness entered the race. It spread through all Adam's children and has revealed itself in every culture on the earth. All the religions of the world reflect the desperate desire to solve the problem of the orphan spirit. Whether it is appeasing the gods of polytheism, denying fatherhood in pantheism and naturalism, or debating the nature of God in monotheism, religion is obsessed with orphans seeking a way to get back into the garden where fellowship and partnership with Father God was real.

Israel, The Second Son of God

The Genesis account goes on to tell how God the Father's strategy for restoring a relationship with orphans began with calling another son to his side. He made a covenant with Abraham that would result in a people God would call his son. The descendants of Abraham would dwell in slavery (a picture of fatherlessness) for four hundred years. God tabbed a man named Moses to lead them into a land reminiscent of Eden. He treated them like sons. By miraculous means he delivered them from Egypt. He provided food from heaven's kitchen. He fought their enemies allowing them to partner with him. He gave them his laws for guaranteeing success and significance in the world. They were obviously favored among the nations. They were the "son" of God (Exodus 4:22-23).

But they were children of Adam first. Still harboring the fatherless mentality they inherited from Adam, they could not embrace the privileges and responsibilities of being the son of God the Father. Israel exposed its orphan heart. Worried about provision, they ignored the laws of rest and celebration (Sabbath and feasts). Fearful of stronger nations, they compromised their loyalty and made treaties with the Father's enemies. Needing to find significance in their isolation, they turned laws into walls that would separate and define them as superior to other nations. Like all orphans, they were controlled by the fleshly perspective. Self-focused and survival-oriented, they developed a religion that was a far cry from the one the Father had given them.

In the account of Abraham and his two sons, we can see a picture of the difference between sons of the flesh and sons of the Father. God had promised to Abraham and Sarah a son who would be the Seed and who would bring about the restoration of fallen creation (Genesis 12:1-3). There was a long delay, so they began to worry that it wasn't going to happen. They concocted a scheme whereby they could have an heir who would fulfill the promise. Abraham, with Sarah's permission, had a son, Ishmael, by Sarah's servant, Hagar. He was the fruit of Abraham and

Sarah's worry, doubt, and scheming to accomplish, in their own strength, what God had promised to do for them. This is flesh in action!

God did not accept this son as the one he promised. Though Abraham and Sarah had no strength to produce a child, Isaac was born miraculously, fulfilling the promise of God the Father. He was a symbol of the Son of the Spirit. Isaac grew up in the household of Abraham. He was fathered by Abraham. He knew he was a son with significance. Ishmael on the other hand, was cast out of the household. He was isolated and wandered in the land. He was called a "wild donkey" of a man. He is the picture of the orphan spirit. He lives independently, jealous of the son. He persecutes the son.

The nation of Israel came through Isaac. It was his children and grandchildren that became the heroes of the nation called the people of God. There was natural conflict between the sons of Isaac and the sons of Ishmael. One represented the son. The other represented the orphan.

By the time Jesus was born, the nation of Israel had become more like Ishmael than Isaac. In fact, when the Apostle Paul explained the persecution the Jews were raising against the Christians, he revealed the true identities intended in the Old Testament types of Isaac and Ishmael (Galatians 4:21-31). Israel had become Ishmael, and the disciples of Jesus were Isaac. The issue of sonship is definitely spiritual and not natural. [Sonship is a matter of a spiritual, not a natural, relationship.]

Jesus, The Third Son of God

Since Adam there had not been a complete model of a son. All the types and shadows of the Old Testament kept the concept alive, but they were imperfect. Finally, there came a Son who demonstrated what life looked like when the Father and Son relate properly. He was more conscious of the Father than of his own flesh. He had no worry because he knew implicitly that the whole estate belonged to him. He had no permanent house to call home. Even the foxes had more physical security than he. The birds had nests; he had no place to lay his head. But he could not worry because he was the Son, and he knew it. The Jews controlled by the orphan spirit tried to kill him, but they couldn't. He was under the protection of the Father. Their spies could not find him and their swords would not cut him until the Father said so. When he had need of some physical entity he simply requested it. When it was suggested that he owed a temple tax, he told Peter to get it from the mouth of a nearby fish. When he needed lunch to feed a multitude, he used one from a small boy. When he needed a donkey to ride into Jerusalem, he conscripted one from across town. When he needed a tomb as a place to wait for his resurrection, he borrowed one.

He was not interested in starting a new religion or building new temples, but he was intent on displaying the nature of the Father/Son relationship. Everything he did demonstrated what eternal life looks like. Finally, through his death and resurrection, he procured that life for those who would believe in him.

Christians, The Sons of God on Earth

The greatest invitation ever offered comes from the Father to the orphaned sons of Adam. Through the life, death, resurrection, and ascension of Jesus the Son, we can be restored to the original design. We can have the same relationship with the Father that Jesus had. We can have the same consciousness of the Father that Jesus enjoyed. He demonstrated it during his life and he procured it through his death and resurrection. From the cross he declared the anguished cry of the orphan, "My God . . . why have you forsaken me?" He became the orphan so we could become the sons of God. Now we no longer have to strive to get back to the Father. There is no price to pay or regulations to keep that will qualify us. We are declared "sons of God" by none other than the Father himself.

But that is not all! Not only are we declared sons of God, but he has sent the Spirit of adoption into our hearts so that our relationship is experiential as well as legal. We know that we are sons of God at a level deeper than emotion and higher than the intellect. His Spirit testifies with our spirit that we are sons of God. Now the challenge is to believe this great news. It means we must abandon our fatherless thinking and embrace the mercy given to us by the Father. It will take some time to complete our repentance, but it is time we got started. There is a world to subdue in partnership with Father.

2. The Radical Revelation

After creation, the first radical change on the earth was related to mankind's sin. It was a terrible change. Adam and Eve had been created to enjoy the Father completely and to partner with him in discovering the world's mysteries as they developed creation. But they were enticed by the tempter, who insinuated they were seeing incompletely. He lied when he promised them a new and better perspective. When Adam and Eve sinned their eyesight was affected all right – it was perverted. Where they once could see God as Father, they were now afraid of him. Where they were once more conscious of relating to God in the spirit, they were now preoccupied with their flesh. They were now so conscious of the natural, physical, and personal that spiritual reality became cloudy and secondary. Since the physical, natural, and personal became primary, they interpreted the world from that perspective. This is the first description of "the flesh" that continues to battle against the spiritual reality.

In his last discourse with his disciples, Jesus explained to them how he came to restore relationship with the Father. He had spent approximately 33 years on earth demonstrating the true nature of God the Father. He was about to finish the work necessary for their restoration to take place. He tells them in John 14 that he is going to the Father to prepare them a place in the Father so they can have the relationship he has with the Father.

Four of the disciples respond to Jesus explanation. Together they give us a clue that they didn't really understand what he was saying. Like the rest of mankind, they were orphans and could not see what the Son was telling them. They still had Adam's eyes and were peering from behind a bush trying to keep the fig leaves in place. Peter couldn't conceive of where Jesus was going. Thomas contended that contrary to Jesus' statement, he didn't know where or how to get there. Phillip asserted that if they could just have a visitation like Moses or Isaiah they would be satisfied. Judas was baffled by the very thought of Jesus being real to them but not to the world. These all reflect similar perspectives common to us all.

First, there was Peter who demanded to know where Jesus was going. Jesus told him that it was somewhere he couldn't go. Peter was sure he was committed enough to go anywhere with Jesus, that he would fight and die for the one he believed in. But like all orphans he was not aware of his own inner fears. Jesus gave him the good news that he would be exposed. It really is good news! We can never deal with our state until we know how deeply we have been affected by sin. It would take more than the full commitment of Peter's flesh to stand the test that was coming. But, once exposed, Peter could, through repentance, find the eyes to see from a son's perspective. It is a good thing to find that we are approaching life from a fatherless mentality. There is a cure for that because God has acted to fix that problem. As we shall see, it is a matter of believing in the Son who reveals the Father.

Then there was Thomas, who couldn't grasp Jesus' destination or his direction. He was looking for a place in the created order while Jesus was speaking of a place in the uncreated Father. Limited by his natural, physical and personal eyes, he could not comprehend that the goal of life is to be in the Father. Jesus answered the big questions for him. It is very likely that Thomas was looking for some instructions about how to walk the right path, but Jesus made it clear you must know where you are going before you can choose the path.

Some have concluded that the destination is heaven. They are looking for a physical place where peace reigns and pleasures are abundant. This of course fits into the mentality of the flesh-minded orphan. More of the good stuff and none of the bad stuff – it must be heaven. It must be a place far away from earth, because earth holds too many memories of lack and pain.

Others are pointed toward success. In an "orphanic" (new word) world, success is measured by symbols that speak of achievement, affirmation, and affection. Riches, titles, trophies, toys, memorials, and resumes fill the lives of those who pursue success. And ambition, aggression, commitment, and communication skills are the way to succeed. In a phrase: learning how to work the world's system.

Still others are working toward being better. There are lots of paths to be better: Meditation, medication, managing skills, coping techniques, more knowledge, etc.

But if someone is going to the Father, there is only one way, that is through the Son. Great teachers can help us along the path of knowledge. Skilled psychologists can help us tread the path of self-understanding. Religious leaders can help us develop a behavioral righteousness that appears satisfactory. But only the Son can introduce us to the Father. Yes, it is exclusive, but God has never apologized about being exclusive. He chose only one nation and he allowed only Levi's family to be priests. He is not trying to satisfy our distorted sense of egalitarianism. Jesus is gloriously exclusive in an inclusive way. Anyone who comes to the Father through believing the Son is welcome. There are no ethnic, social, legal, gender, or geographic boundaries; just faith in the Son!

Many would like to approach God without a mediator. They don't get it. Orphans cannot just walk into the inheritance without mediation. Only Jesus the Son has become an orphan for Adam's race. He was separated from the Father on the cross so that we would never have to be separated from him again. Lots of religious people like to think that they can have a relationship with God without going through Jesus. They may have a relationship with a god of their own creation, but only the Son can make a place for them in the Father.

What does the destination look like? The Father's house is a place in relationship with him that allows us a place at his table. We sit there because we are sons. We did nothing to gain the place, and we do nothing to keep it. We also have a son's perspective on reality. Like Jesus, the Son, we are more conscious of the Father than of trying to secure our provision, protection, and promotion.

Jesus is the truth about reality. Only he has a clear view of both God and mankind. And this clarity extends to his view of money, trouble, service, suffering, and glory. He is truth, not just a teacher who offers truth. He is reality. When we discover that we are in him, we are finally in reality. In fact, he is also life. The eternal life that everyone wants is nothing less than Jesus revealing the Father and granting us the privilege of living in full fellowship with the Godhead.

Before we finish with Thomas, we should note that Jesus promised him from now on he would know the destination and the direction. Something as dramatic as the fall of mankind was taking place. Jesus was restoring to Adam's race the right to see reality accurately and to live eternally. Thomas had seen Jesus but didn't know what he saw. He was about to, and he would be radically changed.

Then there was Philip, who wanted to have a special visitation. He had heard Jesus tell Thomas that he was going to see the Father, and he wanted that experience. He remembered how such visitations had impacted Moses, Isaiah, and Ezekiel. He figured that if he could have one of those it would satisfy him totally. But Jesus was the full visitation. All others, though effective, were partial and incomplete. Jesus was the living vision so that seeing him would have transforming effects. He was and is the exact representation of God. It would take special eyes to see this, but that blessing was on the way.

Jesus lived out in human terms the life of a son of God. His perspective was dominated by spiritual reality. Since God is the Father of spirits, those who worship him must do so in spirit and truth. Jesus was not apologetic about his physical body, nor was he ashamed of the natural world, but he made his decisions based on input from the spiritual realm. He was not spooky, but he was supernatural. He told Philip that his (Jesus') works and his words were consistently revealing the nature of the Father and the Son. Any unprejudiced eyes could have seen it, but, of course, Philip was an orphan and needed an eye transplant.

The new perspective would come on the day the Helper came. The Spirit sent from the Father would come and make it real for the followers of Jesus.

I will not leave you as orphans; I will come to you. Yet a little while and the world will see me no more, but you will see me. Because I live, you also will live. In that day you will know that I am in my Father, and you in me, and I in you.

John 14:18-20 (ESV)

Notice the four aspects of the coming. One: **"I will come to you."** We will be conscious of the presence of Jesus and the Father. This is consistent with God's intention all along since he never meant for his people to live without his presence. That is why the temple was so important for Israel. It was where God's presence met earth. Now Jesus is saying that the temple will be the disciples both corporate and individual. Like Adam in the Garden and Jesus on earth, we can live so conscious of the Father's presence that our fleshly component cannot dominate.

Two: **"you will see me."** Here we get the new perspective. Now, because the gospel opens our eyes, we can finally see spiritual reality.

And even if our gospel is veiled, it is veiled only to those who are perishing. In their case the god of this world has blinded the minds of unbelievers, to keep them from seeing the light of the gospel of the glory of Christ, who is the image of God.

2 Corinthians 4:3-4 (ESV)

Notice that the gospel reveals the true nature of God, that he is Spirit and Father. The Helper will open our eyes to see what sin has blinded us to. We can now enjoy being sons who do not run away in fear of God, but run towards him in love.

Three: **"you also will live."** Actually Jesus said, "Because I live, you also will live." The same life he demonstrated on earth will be transferred to his own believers. They will know what it means to live with open eyes seeing reality again. They will be conscious of the unconditional love of the Father. They will want to display his glory to all creation. After all, they will know that they are sons.

Four: **"you will know."** They will know that they are intertwined in the relationship of the Father and the Son. This knowledge is beyond the reasons of the mind and the emotions of the soul. It is that spiritual knowledge that cannot be explained yet is more real than thought. We are now getting an education for eternity when we will know as we are known. How are we known by God? He knows us in spirit.

From now on, therefore, we regard no one according to the flesh. Even though we once regarded Christ according to the flesh, we regard him thus no longer.
2 Corinthians 5:16 (ESV)

We might as well get used to it now, because this is the real world.

Judas is the last of the four disciples who responded to Jesus. He can't grasp how Jesus can be real to the disciples and not to the rest of the world. Again we see here the confusion of the orphaned mind. The physical world is so real while the spiritual world is so vague. But Jesus gives the answer: Those who love him will become the host of the presence of God in Jesus and the Father. The key to this kind of love is in believing the word of Jesus. It is somewhat strange because his word is not exactly what the physical eyes see. It will take some trust in the person of Christ. Surely he would not deceive. Believing his word depends on trusting him. When we do, we are the recipients of a radical revelation.

3. Abba Conscious

During his last discourse with his disciples, Jesus promised them that he would not leave them as orphans but would instead send the Helper to make real to them the same relationship he had with the Father (John 14:18-20). They would become conscious that Jesus is in the Father, that they were in Jesus, and that Jesus was in them. This was an amazing promise, as radical a thought as had ever been in their minds. Was Jesus really saying that they could have the same sense of intimacy with the Father as Jesus had? Was he sharing with them the fellowship enjoyed by the Godhead?

Jesus' promises were fulfilled during the annual celebration of the Feast of Pentecost. Those gathered began to see some strange phenomena, physical signs that pointed to a greater reality. First, they heard the sound of a mighty wind. Wind had often been used to describe the movement of the Spirit of God, and Jesus himself had used wind as a metaphor to describe the essential nature of the kingdom of God (John 3:1-8). The wind they heard was signaling the restoration of mankind to the reality of the spirit world. Adam and Eve had enjoyed walking with God who is Spirit, but they had lost that clear sense of the world beyond the natural. Spiritual reality had become cloudy and secondary. Only sporadically had mankind been able to access this realm, so there was much speculation and confusion about how the physical and spiritual realms related. From the day they heard this rushing, mighty wind, they would be led by the Spirit and not controlled by the circumstances of the physical world.

Tongues of fire sat upon each believer. Fire had been a symbol of God's presence for centuries. When God gave Moses the Law, the mountains were on fire. Before that, when God made a covenant with Abraham, his presence was a smoking fire pot (Genesis 15:12-21). Now the presence of God was on each believer and not just with the Jewish nation. Each believer in Christ would be a temple of the Spirit and could worship anywhere, anytime.

They were also speaking in languages they didn't know. Everyone was hearing the proclamation of the gospel in his or her own language. This was a reversal of the language confusion that God had caused when people tried to build a tower to heaven – the tower of Babel – for the sake of their own name. Now there would be restored communication so that believers could know in the spirit as well as in the natural.

Then another radical thing happened: Peter demonstrated how the Old Testament should be interpreted. Joel, who was one of the revered Old Testament prophets, had spoken of the day when God would intervene and establish a new order. He had used prophetic language depicting the event in cosmic drama.

And it shall come to pass afterward, that I will pour out my Spirit on all flesh; your sons and your daughters shall prophesy, your old men shall dream dreams, and your young men shall see visions; Even on the male and female servants in those days I will pour out my Spirit. And I will show wonders in the heavens and on the earth, blood and fire and columns of smoke. The sun shall be turned to darkness, and the moon to blood, before the great and awesome day of the Lord comes. And it shall come to pass that everyone who calls on the name of the Lord shall be saved...

Joel 2:28-32 (ESV)

Before this New Testament interpretation, most of the Jews had looked for physical and natural fulfillment of this prophecy. Now Peter was introducing what the new creation would look like. The spiritual meaning of everything would take precedence over the natural. The Old Testament writers had been writing about spiritual reality all along, and now its day had arrived. The Spirit had come to make the relationship with the Father a conscious reality. The "seeing" that Adam had lost in the Garden was being restored.

Later the apostle Paul spoke of this new creation dynamic as he explained to the church at Rome what the kingdom of God was all about.

> *For all who are led by the Spirit of God are sons of God. For you did not receive the spirit of slavery to fall back into fear, but you have received the Spirit of adoption as sons, by whom we cry 'Abba! Father! The Spirit himself bears witness with our spirit that we are children of God, and if children, then heirs—heirs of God and fellow heirs with Christ, provided we suffer with him in order that we may also be glorified with him.*
>
> Roman 8:14-17(ESV)

I believe there are at least five aspects of this "Abba-consciousness." We can see these first in the Garden of Eden and then in Jesus who is the last Adam.

First, there is the consciousness of **presence**. Adam had enjoyed the unhindered presence of God before sin intruded. Since that time mankind has been trying to find a way back to the presence of God. The whole Old Testament story is about Israel being the distinct people whose God was present with them. He lived in a tent like they did. Then they built a temple where he met with them in the Holiest place. The whole sacrificial system was about bridging the gap between God and mankind. For centuries Jews dreamed of a day when they could again approach God and be in his presence. That day finally came!

Some are still convinced that it is a dream for the future. They visualize heaven as the only place where mankind can live in the presence of God. But according to the New Testament, heaven starts the day one places his or her trust in Jesus as the only mediator between God and man. Heaven is the unfiltered presence of divine life. John reminds us that eternal life is knowing God the Father and the Son he sent (John 17:3). To imagine heaven as a desirable place without Jesus being the center is to fantasize outside of biblical revelation. One cannot come to the Father unless introduced by the Son. It is popular today for people to profess they have a relationship with God, but not Jesus. They think his claims of being the only way are ridiculous. They are sure they have bridged the gap by being sincere and authentic. There are many gods out there which are products of man's projections, but the God who created everything and who will consummate everything is a Father and can be known only through the Son who became the ultimate sacrifice for sin.

I was saddened recently when a prominent sports figure in this country declared that he was embracing Torah because he believed you had to get to know the Father before you can know the Son. He had it backwards. You can't know the Father except through the Son. And the Spirit has come to dwell in us to make that relationship conscious.

The second aspect of the Abba-conscious life is **pleasure**. God actually has pleasure in his sons, just as Adam and Eve enjoyed the presence and pleasure of the Father and he obviously enjoyed them. God tried to get Israel to believe that he delighted in them, but they just couldn't comprehend it. They continued to drift off to other gods that promised them pleasure. And they were afraid of the God who actually enjoyed them.

It is difficult to believe that God enjoys us. When I get up in the morning and look into the mirror, I can't imagine anyone delighting in me. When I think of all the selfish things I have done, I can only imagine others being repulsed. To believe that the Father actually looks forward to being with me is a stretch. I have been programmed by the orphan's perspective. I can only hope God will tolerate me. If I could actually believe God the Father was anxiously waiting for me to wake up and visit with him, I wonder if that would make me more eager to get up?

Some old friends, guys who played football together in college, got together a few years back in a hunting cabin. We took all the clothing and gear for a few days of man-fun, but we got to talking about each other's lives. We bragged on and prayed for our kids as the hours flew by. We stayed up much too late delighting in each other. We were up before dawn putting on heavy warm clothes, but we began visiting again around the breakfast table. The sun came up, and by the time we noticed it was almost noon. We talked over each other, eager to get our stories in the mix. We laughed and cried. We rehearsed how great we were back when. When the hour to depart arrived, we were all sad, but greatly blessed by a few hours of delight in each other.

How much more does the Father delight in us? Actually, he delights in us exactly the same as he delights in the Son. That is what it means to be a "son of God." Being joint-heirs with Christ means we get what he inherited. It can't mean anything less. Think of how much the Father has eternally delighted in the Son. He created mankind so that someone could enjoy the Son as much as the Father did. There is nothing that delights the Father as much as the Son.

I think we have some mind changing to do.

The third aspect of this consciousness is **purpose**. Adam originally knew his purpose; Jesus knew his purpose; Israel misunderstood their purpose. But we can know ours. Adam was to enjoy the Father and partner with him in developing creation. In short, he was to glorify God, to make his nature known in the earth. Israel was to be a son of God glorifying him on earth by representing him as a forgiving Father. Jesus revealed his purpose in his "high-priestly prayer:"

> *I glorified you on earth, having accomplished the work that you gave me to do...I have manifested your name to the people whom you gave me out of the world.*
> John 17:4, 6a (ESV)

Could that be our purpose also? Well, of course. Only an orphan could possibly conceive of life apart from partnering with the Father. If we aren't living to glorify him, it doesn't really matter what we do vocationally. In fact, if we *are* living to glorify him it really doesn't matter very much what we do. Of course, we will gravitate to our skills and gifts, but the real issue is making his name known to those around us and developing the plot in the garden we were given.

In an atmosphere of meaninglessness, purpose is difficult to find. When people are taught that they are products of random chance and that all truth is relative to the individual, there is little to give us clues about purpose. But when we believe we are sons of God destined to make his name known in the earth, we can rise to the occasion and make a difference during our time here. There are mysteries to be solved and treasures to be discovered in this creation. The sons of God will enjoy working with the Father in fulfilling his purpose for creation no matter where they are assigned.

The fourth aspect of Abba-consciousness is **provision**. This is the area that trips us up so often. As orphans we tend to worry about our needs being met. Adam had plenty of food on every tree in the garden. Israel had received manna from heaven as a display of the Father's intention to provide for them. Jesus was confident that when he needed something to carry out his assignment, it would be there. There was a lunch when he needed to feed five thousand families. There was a donkey when he needed to make his triumphal entry. There was a tomb when he needed to wait for the resurrection. Today there is a community of faith that will finish the job he began. He has never worried about provision.

One reason we worry is that we live with our assignments disconnected from our provision. We often think of provision in terms of survival or significance. When we haven't identified our assignment clearly, provision becomes the goal rather than the means. We find ourselves "needing" things to affirm our success, so we gather our symbols of success and display them, hoping for some sense of significance. Then we hoard things for fear that the supply will not always be there.

It seems that our greatest worries come from the perceived lack of resources because we have not connected our needs with our assignments. When I disconnect my need for clothes, food, travel, comfort, and convenience from my calling, I have trouble believing God is interested. Oh sure, he would provide a boat for me if I were in the tropics and needing to get to an unreached tribe. But is he interested in my needs here in a country with more wealth than any place on earth? Is he embarrassed that I would even expect him to provide for me when there are so many in the world who don't have what I already have? But if I can believe that God's sovereign hand has placed me in this environment to make his name known, maybe I can trust him to grant me the resources to get that done.

Our Father has not been miserly in his provision. He has given us the same Spirit that raised Jesus from the dead. Why, then, shouldn't he give new life to the hopeless: restore a marriage, or a church, or a relationship to new life? If he can defeat death, maybe he can also defeat bitterness and addiction. When we are conscious of his abundant provision, we are liberated from worry and fear. When we are aware of his provision, we can work with confidence.

The fifth aspect of the Abba-conscious life is **protection**. Adam had the angels surrounding the Garden of Eden. Israel had God's covenant that he would fight their enemies. Jesus could call 10,000 angels at any time. We too are in the Father's hand, and no one can snatch us from it.

There were several times in Jesus' earthly life that people tried to kill him. He was able to simply walk away. He moved through these crises with confidence because, in his words, his "time had not come." The Father was in charge of the events of his life regardless of how powerful the Roman government was or how bitter the Jewish leaders had become. No one could touch him until his time. Likewise, we are indispensable until our assignment is done. We are not walking the tightrope of survival wondering if accidents or terrorists are going to prevail. We are in the hands of the Father, who is bigger and stronger than any and all. And when he determines our assignment is done, he will decide how we transition from this world. His promise is sure. He has prepared a place in the Father for us and we can enjoy it now. When death comes, we will continue to enjoy the consciousness of the Father that we are getting accustomed to now.

By his death and resurrection Jesus made it possible for us to be sons of God. It is already a legal fact based on the justice of God, but there is more. We are not only sons of God legally, but we have also been given the Spirit of adoption that makes us conscious of the relationship. Eternal life is visceral as well as legal. At a level deeper than emotion and higher than intellect, we know we are sons of God.

4. Driven By Flesh or Led By the Spirit

Christians who are serious about living out their faith are often heard describing their battle with the flesh. They often lament how often they lose the fight against such things as lust, fear, greed, selfishness, lying, resentment, etc. It seems the battle rages constantly, and we often lose because we can't identity the real enemy. We are grateful that our gracious Father forgives us, but we grow tired of failure and even become embarrassed to come to him again.

Various methods have been tried against the flesh. We have tried suppressing the flesh, and that doesn't work for long. Our will becomes weak, and eventually we give in to an impulse that seems to have a life of its own. We sometimes try casting out the demons in hope of final liberation, only to discover that flesh cannot be cast out. It must be crucified. Denial is another option. It's preferred option when nothing else seems to work. We simply conclude that we don't have a battle and ignore it. Eventually, though, we get tired of being controlled by the baser impulses of our lives and venture out of denial.

So, what is the flesh? **Flesh is the perspective and approach of the orphan trying to make sense of life.** Remember what happened in the Garden of Eden. When Adam and Eve sinned their perspective changed. They defined reality in terms of providing for themselves, protecting themselves, and promoting themselves. Afraid of God, they were fixated on covering their

25

shame and justifying their actions. They viewed life as orphans, and this is the origin of the "flesh." Flesh produces some ugly works, some of which the apostle Paul listed for us:

> *Now the works of the flesh are evident: sexual immorality, impurity, sensuality, idolatry, sorcery, enmity, strife, jealousy, fits of anger, rivalries, dissensions, divisions, envy, drunkenness, orgies, and things like these.*
>
> Galatians 5:19-21a (ESV)

I have heard some in-depth biblical word studies done of this list, but just knowing what the words mean doesn't seem to help eliminate their reality. We might find some solace in discovering that we don't produce all of the flesh-works, or that there are worse flesh-works than ours. But until the flesh is dead, the works will continue one way or the other.

Flesh has become the default mode for mankind. It is often demonstrated in the stories of the Old Testament. Even Abraham, the father of faith, had trouble with it. God promised him that he would have a son who would ultimately produce a seed that would bless (instead of curse) the nations. Time passed, and there was no son. As he closed in on 100 years and his wife Sarah neared 90, they began to doubt the promise. So they schemed to produce a son. Hagar the slave girl would bear Abraham a son, and by a technicality in the law, he would have an heir.

Abraham's problem began when he perceived God's promise as an instruction. He felt responsible to produce what God said he would give him. Flesh is like that. It drives. When things are not working out, it will scheme to find a way. It cannot tolerate "failure" or even delay. The orphan mind cannot afford to be unproductive. That might threaten acceptance. So the unmet needs inside produce a pressure to move, make something happen, produce.

The product of Abraham and Sarah's plan was their son Ishmael. He is the Old Testament picture of the orphan's life. He was cast out of Abraham's home and wandered in isolation. He became angry and jealous. He and his mother were a source of persecution to Isaac. He felt victimized and vulnerable and became competitive to the point of criminality. He produced a people of hostility. He had lots of land but no sense of being an heir.

It is worthwhile to mention that there is a vast difference in a son's inheritance and an orphan's riches. An inheritance is a stewardship that is connected to the past and the future. It is a trust that must be handled according to a purpose greater than we alone can give it. People who are aware of being heirs don't consider their resources as ultimately their own. They are very conscious of using everything to fulfill the purpose for which it was passed down to them. An orphan's riches on the other hand are a collection of things used as symbols of success and idols for security. Money always trips them up. Absent a clear purpose and sense of destiny, they will become victims of greed and fear.

We've noted before that Israel became like Ishmael and demonstrated flesh when it dons religious garb. Flesh will craft a religious system that is literal because the orphan's perspective is primarily on the physical and natural. It will be legalistic because rules are the only way to govern behavior when you don't have a vital relationship with the Father. It will be litigious, since being right on the details is important to one whose significance is based on performance.

Like the original Ishmael, this fleshy religion promotes victimization. No one really understands the orphan and he capitalizes on it. He is more comfortable when in the minority, nursing his wounds. He demands respect and uses his mistreatment as leverage to get his way. He is very proud of outward symbols of success and is devastated when they are threatened or taken away. (Is this a description of Israel in Jesus' day and thousands of lifeless church-goers today?)

Those caught in this system are always looking for more instructions. In the absence of life, instructions seem to offer a chance to succeed. These folks are also zealous in their efforts to gain adherents to the group, not for the new adherents' benefit, but to authenticate the system. The more they can gather into their group, the more they are convinced that they are right, and being right is very important. Living by a "flesh-perspective" is inherently frustrating. Driven by unmet needs, addicted to perform for acceptance, feeling responsible for meeting our own needs of provision, protection and permanence, and constantly fighting fear of failure and punishment, we grow tired and angry.

Flesh is the default mode for all mankind. It can be managed by religious systems, but it can only be defeated by death. That is why Jesus the Son came and took on the fleshly body of mankind and experienced the separation from the Father that we orphans deserve. When he died on the cross the soldiers crucified him, but he crucified the flesh's dominance over those who came to him. He then sent the Spirit to indwell the believer so that we could be led by the Spirit rather than driven by our flesh. Paul describes this, too:

> *But I say, walk by the Spirit, and you will not gratify the desires of the flesh.*
>
> Galatians 5:16 (ESV)

Note that the text does not say, "do not gratify the desires of the flesh and you will walk in the Spirit." That reverses the order. Only as we are led by the Spirit to experience intimacy with the Father and enjoy the Son's inheritance will we ever be willing to give up the flesh. Until there is a legitimate alternative we will always yield to the perspective of the flesh and therefore produce its works. The Spirit is stronger than the flesh and will produce certain fruit. It will be obvious, to those who can see, whether one is living as an orphan or as a son.

> *But the fruit of the Spirit is love, joy, peace, patience, kindness, goodness, faithfulness, gentleness, self-control; against such things there is no law. And those who belong to Christ Jesus have crucified the flesh with it passions and desires.*
>
> Galatians 5:22-24 (ESV)

It is sadly possible to actually be a son and continue to think like an orphan. Spiritual people can operate in the flesh – but they don't have to. Someone has said, "Flesh is anything we use to make life work without trusting the Spirit of God." We can become good at finding the substitutes and baptizing them into our system. Hopefully we will soon tire of the fleshy works and run to the Father who sent the Spirit to make our sonship real.

The question is how? How do we access this life of being led by the Spirit rather than driven by the flesh? Jesus demonstrated what a man filled with the Spirit does. First he rests in his relationship with the Father. Conscious of being unconditionally loved, he is free to explore all the creative impulses in his heart. Confident in the Father's purpose, he uses every gift to fulfill that purpose. Jesus fulfilled all the roles foreshadowed in the Old Testament where men were anointed by the Spirit. He was the *king* of all God's realm, ruling over everything except God the Father himself. He was the ultimate *priest* since he alone became the mediator between God and man. He was also the complete *prophet* who delivered the full message of God to all of creation.

So Jesus was conscious of his place with the Father and simply acted out of that consciousness. He never tried to do anything to gain position. He was comfortable being the Son of the Father.

Is it now possible for us to live as Jesus did? We have been regenerated by the Spirit. That includes being alive to God in a way that those "in the flesh" are not. The death that separated mankind from God in the Garden has been overcome by the Spirit. The Spirit gives life to our dead spirits so that we are alive to God. We can relate to the Father of spirits. We have been given the capacity to see the kingdom of God in a way we could not before. But not only have we been regenerated, we have received the Spirit of Adoption. That means we actually are conscious of being related to God as Father. God is no longer an unknowable sovereign who demands righteousness. He is our Father, and we know it in the deepest part of our being. But there is more. He has gifted us as members of the body of Christ on earth. We have abilities, that when used in mutual submission to other gifted sons, will promote the Kingdom of God and glorify the Father.

Since the Spirit leads, we must simply follow. That is what "led" people do! In an effort to discover what that looks like, let's look at three words:

The first word is **perspective**. We must take advantage of the new position we have been given. We are no longer orphans wandering in the wilderness without clear purpose or destiny. We stand in grace.

> Therefore, since we have been justified by faith, we have peace with God through our Lord Jesus Christ Through him we have also obtained access by faith into the grace in which we stand and we rejoice in hope of the glory of God.
>
> Romans 5:1-2 (ESV)

Imagine that you are a 16 year-old orphan and you have lived your whole life in a poorly-run orphanage. You have never had quite enough food. You have had no possessions of your own. Even your clothes could be taken by others when you were not wearing them. One day a kind, wealthy, fatherly man picks you up and informs you that he has legally adopted you. He shows you the papers and assures you that nothing can reverse your legal position as his child and heir. He then takes you to his home. As you enter he shows you the kitchen with two large refrigerators filled with food. There is a well-stocked pantry. He says that you can eat whenever you are hungry. There are keys lying on the counter. He says they are for your car. He takes you up the stairs and shows you your own room, actually a suite with a large bed, desk, computer, large-screen TV, and a closet with clothes just your size for every occasion.

What would you do? Would you need a manual to tell you that stealing food and stuffing it beneath your pillow would not be tolerated? Would you need reminding that putting your clothes in bed with you while you slept was frowned upon? No, you would just need to stand there awhile and get your bearings. When it began to sink in where you were standing, the deviant behavior would cease to be a problem.

We can't make too much of our need to have a son's perspective rather than the default orphan mentality. The gospel must be preached and repeated often. We are so accustomed to living in the orphanage that the new home is foreign to us. There is room for large repentance, changing the way we think and therefore act.

The second word is **power**. We are indwelt by the same Spirit that raised Jesus from the grave, so there is hope for transformation. He can change things that we could never change without him. He can heal scars from the past and can break addictions to substitutes and replace them with passion for God's glory. He can resurrect love and initiate forgiveness. Actually, there is nothing sin causes that the Spirit cannot radically reverse because he lives in us and works through us.

The third word is **process**. The Holy Spirit leads us by exposing our dependency upon substitutes and showing us what is real. He opens our eyes to the reasons we can't control our temper or our lusts. He is not embarrassed when we reveal that we live according to the thinking pattern of the flesh. He exposes it so that we can by faith access the grace that replaces it. We don't have to live in denial when we know that he is actually leading us into those situations that will reveal the bushes we hide behind. Then we get to make a choice: we can believe what God says about us and the situation, or we can continue to play the orphan game. Like Israel when they were led to the edge of Canaan, we have the option to take what is promised or yield to fear because of the obstacles our eyes behold. Whatever we choose will determine the level of joy we experience afterward. We can move forward trusting his word and seeing his marvelous works of faithfulness in our behalf, or we can take another wandering trip around the wilderness. But be assured he will not stop exposing until we respond.

It is indeed a journey. None of us gets rid of the orphan perspective completely at the beginning. We walk our paths of discovery knowing that there is so much more of the inheritance than we have yet seen. Our hope escalates and our faith is tried. We are partners with our Father, and the Holy Spirit continues to reveal to us what an unimaginable privilege that really is. We continue to be exposed so that he can be revealed. The flesh is a real dynamic, but it is defeated by the Spirit sent by the Father and the Son.

5. Sons as Heirs

Since we know the single dynamic that drives history is the relationship between Father and Son, it should not surprise us that one of the major themes of Scripture is inheritance. Jesus made it abundantly clear in his last discourse with his disciples that he came to make possible for them a relationship with the Father just like his own. In the new age starting with Pentecost they would be sons and heirs, just like he was before them.

As wonderful as this is, it has never been without conflict. After the day of Pentecost, the early church began to walk out their assignment. They were the representatives of God on the earth, but not everyone understood or agreed. There were many Jews who contended that they were the heirs of God's promise because of their blood connection with Abraham. After the church in Galatia was established, some of these men confused the new believers there by insisting that a proper relationship with God must include Jewish requirements, such as circumcision. Paul, the apostle of the gospel of God, addressed this situation with a letter that answers the question that has caused conflict since the Garden of Eden:

Who is the heir and what is the inheritance?

And if you are Christ's then you are Abraham's offspring, heirs according to promise.
Galatians 3:29 (ESV)

And because you are sons, God has sent the Spirit of his
Son into our hearts, crying, "Abba! Father!" So you are
no longer a slave, but a son, and if a son then an heir
through God.

                                               Galatians 4:6-7 (ESV)

Adam was the first son and heir. He had the privilege of living in the presence and pleasure of the Father as he worked to fulfill his purpose. We could say that he had **presence with partnership**. Mankind was designed to live in the presence of God the Father and, outside that relationship, he is lost. Nothing makes lasting sense. Not knowing God accurately, he doesn't know himself or his environment. He struggles with purpose and with provision.

We too were designed to work with God in subduing the earth. Mankind cannot do that apart from a genuine partnership with God. Limited to our observational perspective we cannot know what is required to fulfill our assignment. We need the knowledge that only comes by revelation from God himself.

Adam also had **property with prospects**. He was given a relatively small piece of ground and told to manage it. The idea was to increase his responsibility as he accomplished the task. He was to raise up children who could expand the Garden until the whole earth was subdued under the authority of God, with men and women as his vice regents. The Garden was just the starting point. He was not supposed to build a fence around it and limit his inheritance to the small area between the rivers.

To jump ahead in history, Israel was also given a relatively small piece of land. They became so obsessed with its boundaries and protecting it that they neglected the original plan to expand until the whole earth had the blessings of God's mercy. Canaan was just the starting point because the whole earth is God's objective.

Let's back up a little in the story. After Adam's descendants made a mess of things, Noah and his sons were God's representatives on earth after the flood. Each of the sons was given a portion. Ham, Shem, and Japheth became the heirs to the purposes of God, but Shem was the one chosen by God to be the heir of the redemptive promise. Not everyone was happy with the choice.

Abraham had two sons, but there was a controversy about the inheritance. Ishmael received a special blessing and became a leader of many people with great wealth, but Isaac was the heir to God's purpose of redemption. Not everyone was happy.

Isaac had two sons who battled over the inheritance. Jacob traded Esau out of his birthright and tricked him out of his blessing. The line of promise went through Jacob and not Esau. Not everyone was happy.

Jacob had twelve sons. There was an issue of the heir's identity and the nature of the inheritance. Joseph was not the firstborn, but he was the father's favorite. Joseph's sons, Manasseh and Ephraim, were accepted by Jacob as his own sons, even though they were really Jacob's grandsons. Ruben was firstborn, but Judah received the inheritance that would produce the Messiah. Not everyone was happy.

Later, David became king and representative of God's people on earth. He captured all the physical land that God had promised Abraham and established a kingdom that was admired by all the nations. He then transferred his inheritance to his son, Solomon, who was recognized as a worthy heir. After David's death, his sons began a rapid decline, and eventually the kingdom was divided. Both sections were defeated by foreign nations and the physical inheritance was lost. The people longed for a return of David's day. Prophets spoke of a coming day when David's son would regain the inheritance. Even though a remnant returned to Judah from exile to rebuild Jerusalem and the temple, it was a poor substitute for the kingdom they remembered and the one for which they had hoped.

Four hundred years passed before the real heir arrived. He was announced by John the Baptist, the last of the line of Old Covenant prophets. The heir had finally come! But still not everyone was happy.

The Jews wanted him to be a military leader. His disciples wanted him to display his superiority by acts of power. The crowds wanted him to provide bread and entertainment for them. Yet he came as the Son of the Father to make a way for other sons to enjoy the Father the way he does. For approximately 33 years he demonstrated the life of an heir. He enjoyed **presence with partnership**, and **property with prospects**. His "garden" was twelve men he chose to develop. He later told them to go into the whole world with the transforming message of the gospel. It would liberate people so that they could develop their assigned "gardens" to discover the riches and mysteries of creation.

He instructed his disciples that he was leaving so they could fulfill their assignment. He made sure they knew they were the heirs to God's inheritance, and that they would discover all that means by partnership with the Holy Spirit. In fact, on the day of Pentecost when the Holy Spirit came into the believers, Peter identified the promised inheritance as being fulfilled in the Holy Spirit.

And Peter said to them, "Repent and be baptized every one of you in the name of Jesus Christ for the forgiveness of your sins, and you will receive the gift of the Holy Spirit. For the promise is for you and for your children and for all who are far off..."

Acts 2:38-39 (ESV)

Still, not everyone was happy. The Jews still clung to their ancestral link to Abraham as their hope of being heirs. They did not receive Jesus as the heir and conspired in his death. They were no kinder to the apostles and the early church. They were threatened by those who claimed to be heirs of God through Christ.

The inheritance is grand! It is so much more than a small piece of land and a temple. It is the fulfillment of the prototype of Eden, as well as the prototype of Israel in the Promised Land under David. Joint-heirs with Jesus get what he has a right to. They have the same access to the Father. They are loved by the Father in exactly the same way as the Son. They have been given the responsibility to represent the Father on earth with the guarantee of his continual presence and provision. They even get the privilege of suffering with Christ while they wait in eager hope for the full restoration of all creation (Romans 8:17).

Our task is to implement such a privilege. We have grown accustomed to living like outsiders, adept at managing our orphan-like thinking. Yet God has already acted to make us his sons and heirs, so it is now our privilege to believe him and act accordingly. It requires a choice that goes against the grain of our familiar thinking. We are told to "reckon" on what God says and thereby begin to experience its reality. Reckon is an active word denoting a choice we make regardless of accompanying emotions. Simply because God said it, we act on it. Much like the man whose withered hand Jesus healed. Jesus told him to stretch it forth. There was no visible evidence of healing – just Jesus' word. As the man chose to obey, God performed the miracle that allowed him to stretch forth his hand. Even when we think we can't believe, we can choose and God will increase our faith.

We need encouragement from his word and from the community of faith if we are to consistently walk in this inheritance. Its reality can only be known by the revelation of grace. Those who have not been open to God's voice can't understand and they might not be happy, but that can't stop us. We have been given a little with the prospect of a lot more. The whole world is our objective. We want them all to know that the last Adam has come and the garden is once again open.

6. Sons and Suffering

It strikes us as strange that, along with all the wonderful benefits of being heirs of our Father's estate, we are also given suffering. Is that the price we have to pay for the good stuff? Is that what we have to endure to qualify for the blessings of his presence and provision? Why is suffering a part of the wonderful life Jesus has given us? Why didn't God eliminate the painful part and just leave us with all that brings pleasure?

Many who stand opposed to the tenets of Christian theology do so because they can't understand how a good God can permit such pain in his world. They conclude he is either powerless to change things or unconcerned. So they stand in adamant protest against a God they see as less compassionate than themselves. If they were in charge, they think, they would eliminate injustice and suffering. Do we, as Christians, stand helplessly by with no answers to such claims?

The offended heart is not satisfied with an answer; it only wants to accuse. Those who are mad at God for not running things their way can't be convinced of God's goodness by any argument. The scripture has diagnosed them:

> ....So they are without excuse. For although they knew God, they did not honor him as God or give thanks to him, but they became futile in their thinking and their foolish hearts were darkened.
>
> Romans 1:20-21 (ESV)

When they choose not to recognize God as sovereign, they start down a road that leads to no satisfying answers.

We who embrace the scriptures know where suffering came from. We are acquainted with the story of the temptation and fall of mankind. But why did God wait so long to fix the problem? Why didn't he just start over or make a declaration to eliminate the effects of sin?

The Biblical story unfolds God's plan to work through humanity to restore the creation to its original state. Adam was the son who was defeated by Satan's deception, but there would be another Son who would win the battle on the same battlefield on which it was lost. The process would be an unfolding of the very nature of God and the majesty that would never have been exposed without the problem of sin. Through each phase of history, God would be speaking of a reality no one could understand without his explanation.

For instance, the whole episode with Noah reveals that the nature of evil is not primarily external. It can't be eradicated by destruction of external structures. The problem is deeper than infected human and natural structures. The flood pointed ahead to a time in history when a substitute would be judged rather than the created order.

One of the many revelations we gain from Abraham's saga is that it takes time to prepare a people of faith. Within the covenant God made with Abraham was the promise that his descendents would spend 400 years in Egypt in preparation for their deliverance and destiny. They would need to see the mighty hand of their covenant God working for them before they would trust him to lead them to their place and position of representing him in the world.

Moses' story reveals that correct laws will not produce lawful people. The problem with Israel was not a need for better laws. Their own lawless hearts would have to be changed before they could live in covenant with God.

David's kingdom reveals that political purity cannot be sustained in a world of self-obsessed human beings. The kingdom under David was the best possible political structure. The land was enjoying peace, but after David's son, Solomon, things fell apart. The goal is not just getting the right amount of land under control and having the right people in place to govern. The goal is for the ultimate son of David to sit on the throne of God, ruling people whose hearts have been changed to align with the law of God.

The exile of Israel reveals that the old covenant will never work. There must be a new covenant to deal with the root issue. God will have to play the part of both parties in the covenant. He will have to qualify as a man who keeps the requirements and then, as God, bless the man who qualifies.

John the Baptist reveals that God will save the instrument before he saves the world. He was sent to gather the remnant of Israel who would be the first wave of new creation people. Israel would not fail in their mission, though they would need a Savior to accomplish it. Jesus came as the corporate Israelite to do for Israel what they could not do for themselves. It was regenerated Israelites, many first called out by John, who made up the first generation of new covenant believers.

History is a revelation of God's nature showing us One who can, without violating the dignity of man's choice, bring mankind to a place where the original purpose will be fulfilled. Every stage of history was important to the plan. God has been in no hurry and owes no one the right to live without suffering. His plan for restoration is the only hope that there will ever be anything but trouble on the earth. He won't be hurried and will not respond to the foolish chiding of those who think we have the right to demand pleasure. The earth belongs to him. We are his creations. He has already proven his love to be genuine by sending his Son as a substitute for us. Whatever he is doing in preparation to restore all creation is an act of love – no matter how long it takes.

As we see this overall plan of God, we begin to understand why Jesus is the only way to salvation. God would win the battle against Satan by using a man, just like the one who lost it in the Garden. The incarnation was not just a novel idea. It was essential that a man face the same temptations and come out on top. But not just any man. It would be a son of God who could introduce the orphans of the world to the Father. Only a son can show us the Father. He would also have to be the perfect substitute. He could not be an acceptable sacrifice if he were imperfect himself. The problem of the world required a man who is a son and perfect in obedience.

Yet if Jesus did what was necessary to counteract the consequences of sin, why don't we live in a world without sin and its pain? The answer is that he is not finished with the process. We are joint heirs with Jesus and part of the inheritance is to reflect the nature of the Father in a world that still needs to see him. The original purpose of creation was not to ensure a comfortable place for people but to have sons and daughters who would accurately reflect the nature of God to the world. That was also the purpose of Israel's existence. As a nation, they were to reflect the true nature of God to the other nations so that they, too, would want to get back into the Garden with the Father. Now we are called to enjoy sonship with the Father, but we are to be his representatives to those still confused about his nature.

The whole universe is intrigued as it watches this play out. All the angels and principalities of the heavens are waiting to see how God works through mankind to win mankind back to a sonship relationship with God.

> ...so that through the church the manifold wisdom of God might now be made known to the rulers and authorities in the heavenly places. This was according to the eternal purpose that he has realized in Christ Jesus our Lord...
> Ephesians 3:10-11 (ESV)

The devil and his charges have been gloating for centuries about their victory over the son of God. They rejoice in the havoc they have initiated through the selfishness of mankind. They boast about the suffering and pain at work throughout a world created for God's people. But when Jesus died on the cross at the hands of blinded Jews and Romans, the battle was decided. The "man" had won. Now God is allowing time to reveal the implications of that victory.

God believes that love is the strongest power in the universe. He has all power, but has chosen to express it in love. That means that it takes time and opportunities to show the difference in man's power of oppression and God's power of love. In the meantime there are still the manifestations of fallen-ness. The outcome is sure. All creation will be restored. Everything that was affected in the fall of mankind will be restored.

> For I consider that the sufferings of this present time are not worth comparing with the glory that is to be revealed to us. For the creation waits with eager longing for the revealing of the sons of God. For the creation was subjected to futility, not willingly, but because of him who subjected it, in hope that the creation itself will be set free

*form its bondage to decay and obtain the freedom of the
glory of the children of God.*

Romans 8:18-21 (ESV)

Creation groans as it waits for the full culmination of the victory Jesus won through the cross and grave. We, as part of
creation, also groan. Our bodies are not yet redeemed. That full
restoration is as sure as the resurrection, but it remains in our
future. In the meantime we are privileged to display before this
world the difference between sons and orphans. We are intended
to have enemies. It is not our objective to be so relevant to the
world that we lose our distinctions. Jesus said it will be the
persecuted who embrace the kingdom of God.

We hope! We already have the down payment. The presence
of the Holy Spirit is our guarantee that full restoration is ours.
Our hope is a light in a world that has no hope beyond its ability
to observe and compete. We reflect the superiority of our life
when death does not eradicate our joy, when sickness does not
take away our hope. We face the same trials as others, but our
response is different. We are partners with God in demonstrating
the difference between eternal life and ordinary life.

We pray! The greatest leverage we have is our partnership.
We are down here with all the problems, but we have connections
in the heavenlies where all power exists. We can call in the
resources needed to do the will of the Father as the need arises.
And even when we don't know how to pray, the Holy Spirit will
intercede for us. He knows the will of God in every situation. It is
very enlightening to note the prayers the Holy Spirit inspired the
New Testament saints to pray. They center on opening eyes to see
what God has done in Jesus and what that means to us. New
Testament praying looks a lot different than the Old Testament
praying.

Those who prayed the will of God in the old covenant knew that if they were disobeying the agreement, they would be judged and would pay the penalty as prescribed in the covenant. They knew that God had promised if they would repent they could prevent or be delivered from the punishments. Many of their prayers were based on that covenant (e.g. Daniel 9:1ff). In the new covenant the punishments have already been carried out on Jesus and we have been made the sons of God on earth. We need our eyes opened to see the privileges we have. The apostle Paul's prayers reveal his understanding of the covenant in which he lived as well as how important prayer is to accomplishing the given mission. Read them and compare them to your own prayers (Ephesians 1:15ff, 3:14ff).

It is vital that we know where we live in the timeline of history. We are not yet in the culmination phase of history, but we are not in the preparation phase either. We live after the battle has been won and we are privileged to enforce it on earth, waiting for the full revelation of the sons of God and the final restoration of all things.

7. Partnership Explained

The ears of American Christians are not attuned to the sound of the gospel of the New Testament. It is strange to our hearing. Yet there is a growing dissatisfaction with the message that is being marketed as the Christian gospel. As wounded churchgoers cry out, and impotent, crippled men and women grope with broken promises and false hopes, heaven is granting mercy. There is a fresh sound arising, though it is not new at all. It is the old sound of the gospel of the kingdom that shook the world in the first century and has produced transformed lives throughout history. But it seems new to those who have been nourished on a man-centered message which focuses on trying to be better men and women.

Even our recent appreciation for the apostolic gift in the church is evidence that God is granting an awakening to the drowsy church, sick with false hope. The apostle Paul described the apostolic gift as "servants of Christ and stewards of the mysteries of God" (1 Corinthians 4:1). The apostolic gift is most concerned with fully explaining the mysteries of God – the foundational truths that make Christianity distinctive. The gospel is being rediscovered by a generation mesmerized by its majesty.

It is helpful to go back and examine the nature of the New Testament gospel. Two major words describe the gospel. The first is "kerygma," which includes the idea of an announcement so monumental that life will never be the same after the announced event. The other is the word from which we get "evangel," meaning good news. It, too, is an announcement first. Both suggest a proclamation that, if believed, will demand a response. For instance,

> *Now after John was arrested, Jesus came into Galilee, proclaiming the gospel of God, and saying, "The time is fulfilled, and the kingdom of God is at hand…"*
>
> Mark 1:14-15a (ESV)

Anticipating the request for what action this announcement requires, he goes on, "…repent and believe in the gospel" (Mark 1:15b).

Another example is Peter's proclamation at Pentecost. He announces that what they are seeing is a fulfillment of Old Testament prophecy centering around the person of Jesus recently crucified by the will of God and the willful ignorance of man. He then says that this same Jesus has been raised from the dead and made both Lord and Christ. The people hear this proclamation and cry out, "What shall we do?" Then Peter gives the instruction of what is appropriate in response to the announcement.

What is so important about this old story? The focus was on the proclamation first and on the instruction regarding how to respond second. Today the emphasis is on what we should do to get God to respond.

A snapshot of recent history might help us see this dynamic. In the First Great Awakening in the early 18th century, the focus was on the proclamation of the sovereignty of God, the sinfulness of humanity, and the sufficiency of Christ's atonement. One of the major leaders of this great move of God was Jonathan Edwards. His famous sermon, "Sinners in the Hands of an Angry God", was more a proclamation of these truths than an exhortation to action. As he spoke of the awesome justice of God and the more awesome mercy of Christ, hell was seen in its proper place. People began to see themselves as worthy of hell and nothing more. They did not wait for an altar call. They cried out much like the people listening to Peter at Pentecost. This was a general model for the Great Awakening. It had a dramatic impact on the nation, and some say it was the single most powerful influence in preparing the nation for its destiny in the world.

In the latter part of the 18th century and early part of the 19th, there was another awakening. Westward migration was taking place and the atmosphere of optimism regarding man's ability to succeed was strong. The free market was developing and people were measuring their success in terms of growth of wealth and the speed with which it could happen. The tenets of the second awakening readily fit with the mindset of man's focus on making things happen by following certain formulas and schemes.

A major leader of the second awakening was Charles Finny. He concluded that a spiritual awakening was not a miracle as much as the consequence of employing certain means. This made place for the emphasis on persuading people to choose Christ, sometimes even using questionable means to get them to do so. He instituted the inquirer's bench and public prayers for sinners. People were urged to repent and believe, often without a clear announcement of what God has done to elicit such a response. The focus moved from featuring the announcement to featuring the response. Success was often determined by how many attended the meetings and made decisions. Though this movement had many positive results, it is easy to see how this focus aided the industrialization of the gospel and the church.

The effect of this emphasis has been monumental in evangelicalism. The most respected leaders have been those who gather great crowds and have many first-time decisions. Evangelists have been exalted, while pastors and theologians have often been ignored. Church services have taken the form of revival meetings with emphasis on exuberant singing, persuasive preaching, and the altar call. Many of the elements of corporate worship that defined the church for centuries have been ignored or pushed to the side while trying to attract more seekers to the meetings. Fortunes are spent in mass evangelism efforts and television programming.

No one wants to criticize anything that helps people come to know Christ, but some are now looking at the efficiency and effectiveness of this approach to following Christ's command to disciple the nations. We rejoice that an evangelist has spoken to one billion people having one million make a decision for Christ. That is one in one thousand. Statistics show typically 30,000 of the million that responded could be located in any church within three years. All of us who believe in preaching the gospel are thrilled for those who did meet Christ and are living to enjoy his salvation, but the efficiency and efficacy of that approach deserves to be examined.

Then there is the media phenomenon. Billions of dollars are spent by various TV ministries, urging people to push the right button to get God to bless them and make their American dream come true. We cringe when some of these TV personalities are held up as spokesmen for the gospel. It is no wonder that the cry for a fresh look at the gospel has arisen. We have implied that his mercy could be bought with enough self-energized faith and that we could somehow merit his grace by our sincerity and diligence.

So this question begs for an answer: What proclamation is so great that it demands a response? What is it that if believed will change our lives forever? What is the message of the New Testament gospel?

It includes at least the following:

1. God has acted in our behalf by sending his Son to model for us what life looks like when people relate to God as Father; to die in our place, thereby justifying us before God; rising from the grave to grant victory over death; ascending to the right hand of God to rule his kingdom. The Holy Spirit was then sent to make real for us the same relationship with God the Father that Jesus has.

2. He has made us his sons, therefore his representatives on earth. He didn't take us to heaven when we were justified because we have a mission on earth. Like the original Adam, we are to reflect the glory of God on this physical earth. Like Jesus, the last Adam, we can live free from the shame of sin and display the superior nature of the life of love in the face of a fallen world.

3. We live between the ascension of Christ and the full restoration of all things. The gospel always has a time element. Jesus said the fullness of time had arrived with him. Now we live on the "post" side of the cross and the "pre" side of the culmination. For this time we live in hope, because we have been given the down payment of full restoration by the presence of the Holy Spirit. We also live in prayer, with the Spirit helping us to pray when we don't know how. Then we live with persecution because the world is still affected by sin, and we get to display his glory in the midst of it.

4. Already we can think and feel like Adam did before his fall and just as Jesus did while on earth. We have inherited the very life of Jesus the Christ. While we move toward the full restoration of all things defaced by sin, we live as heirs of God, unpacking every day more of the treasure found in Christ.

As one example of the nature of the gospel, let's look at the letter to the Romans. It is Paul's explanation of the gospel as he understands it, and it is first an announcement. For the first five chapters there are no commands or instructions, rather an announcement of what God has done in solving the problem of man's alienation. In chapter six we find some commands. For the first 10 verses he announces what God has done in sending Jesus to die and how that death avails for us so that in Christ we also die to sin and are raised with Christ. He then gives a command: "Reckon yourselves dead to sin and alive to God." Then he goes on to say that because of this new life we can and must yield the members of our body to God and not to sin, since we are no longer slaves to sin.

Then there are no more commands in chapters seven through eleven. Chapter twelve does tell us what the appropriate response is to the magnificent mercy displayed in our behalf. We are to "present [our] bodies as living sacrifices" to God and live that way.

Chapter eight is a masterpiece of announcement. Paul has explained in chapter seven how the law exposed the indwelling sin and left us crying for deliverance from the cycle of sin and death. Chapter eight declares that deliverance. First, there is no condemnation for those in Christ. Then the Spirit has come to replace the cycle of sin and death with life and peace. He also gives us the power to live in the Spirit rather than be controlled by the flesh. We are then told we are heirs of God, joint heirs with Christ. We are partners with God on earth and therefore will be privileged to suffer in that role. We are then encouraged by the declaration that, regardless of the appearance of being defeated, we are undefeatable.

God is for us. If that is so, it doesn't matter who is against us. He is so much for us that he sent his own Son to die for us. Surely this confirms forever that God is not against us. He will go to any length to favor us, and he has unlimited resources.

God chose us before we chose him. And since he started the process, he will complete it. It was his idea that began our relationship, and he has acted through the decisions of mankind to bring history to its predetermined end. He will not be deterred by man's choices, though he never abolishes the dignity he granted to man as his image on earth. He foreknew his own. He predestined them to be conformed to the image of his Son. He called them to himself and gave them faith to believe. He then justified them and guaranteed their safe arrival at the judgment and eternal security in his love. Regardless of the hostile circumstances they may encounter, they will not fail. The same God who gave them faith in the beginning will always have faith for them to endure.

No one can indict God's own. Only God has the right to bring a charge against us, and he is the one who has already declared us justified. Who will condemn us? Jesus alone has the right, but he was condemned in our place so no condemnation remains to be heaped on us. Jesus is also interceding for us now, and there is no accuser who can successfully present a case against us.

Nothing can separate us from the love of God – nothing in this world and nothing in the world to come. Nothing man can think of can alter our standing as sons. Nothing in the demonic world can cause a fracture. His love is the most powerful force in the universe, and it is focused on his own. It will change us. We can't stand in the presence of unconditional love and remain the same. Pressure can move us, but only love will change us. Men may temporarily persuade us beyond our present behavior, but willpower will not change us. So it is no wonder that we are declared "more than conquerors" through him who loved us. The love that was released by God through Jesus at the cross is viral. It cannot be stopped and will not be usurped. It will win every encounter with evil, though appearances may lie.

What an announcement! Who wouldn't want to get in on that? What should we do to embrace this? Repent and believe! Change your mind about God's attitude toward you. You want to believe, so do it. As you believe, you will find your choices changing and your behavior will follow. You are a partner with God; you can now start acting like it.

8. Praying as Sons

With circumstances growing dim, many Christians are calling for more prayer. One might wonder if our main concern is to return to a lifestyle where our creature comforts are restored so we can get on with our self-centered consumerism while watching our retirement funds grow. Often prayer in these situations sounds more like ordering from a fast-food outlet. We spiel off what we want God to do to fix the situation troubling us.

In his last discourse with his disciples, Jesus said that he was going to the Father to prepare a place where his followers would have the same relationship with the Father as he has. In this discussion he recasts prayer:

> *Truly, truly I say to you, whoever believes in me will also do the works that I do; and greater works than these will he do, because I am going to the Father. Whatever you ask in my name, this I will do, that the Father may be glorified in the Son. If you ask me anything in my name, I will do it.*
>
> John 14:12-14 (ESV)

Jesus redefined life for his followers, and part of that redefinition is the nature of prayer.

First, **prayer is a privilege**. Only those who come to God through Jesus have access. It is a common myth that God hears any prayer, no matter who voices it. Of course God hears everything, but he hears the prayers that come in Jesus' name as if Jesus himself is praying them.

It is always interesting to hear people speak of being disap-
pointed with God when they cried out to him in some dire
situation and he didn't answer the way they expected. Some have
spent years angry toward God. They apparently believed all
people have a right to demand things from God. Actually, we
have no rights to approach his throne, because we rebelled against
his order and are barred from access. The only person who has
the right to approach is Jesus the Son. But this is not some
exclusive, elitist doctrine, since anyone is invited to come this
way. There are no racial, geographical, or gender distinctions. All
who will trust Jesus are invited to enter the Father's presence and
make requests. People may pray to other gods without coming
through Jesus, but the God of the Bible can be approached only
through the Son who paid the penalty of man's rebellion. Trying
to approach God apart from faith in Jesus as the mediator is an
attempt to pray based on our own merits.

At this juncture someone usually asks, "what about the Old
Testament saints?" The answer is that they were trusting the God
of mercy, and he was giving them shadows of the Son in the
sacrificial system. As they sacrificed animals and trusted the
priest to intercede for them, they were placing faith in the
shadows of the One who would come as the ultimate priest and
the final sacrifice. They were, therefore, coming to God through
the Son.

This privilege is more than access to God through Jesus'
name. It is the personal communion that is enjoyed in Christian
prayer. Trust is essential to life that has meaning. And living
without trust is a foretaste of hell, which features isolation and
skepticism. Life without faith is boring, but faith in the Father
allows us to enjoy the adventure of bringing the reality of the
kingdom to earth. One who lives daily in faith will experience

many adventures where only God rescues him. You can't read the gospels of the New Testament without seeing how the disciples lived in the midst of an adventure that makes a comic book superhero look tame.

Prayer is talking and listening and waiting in the presence of the Father. What could be more satisfying than visiting with the person who knows everything and who is essentially good? The more we know him, the more we will love him, and that love is the highest form of life. Prayer then is not primarily a duty but the high privilege of sons through Jesus' finished work.

Prayer is also a partnership. One day the disciples asked Jesus to teach them to pray. This is interesting because they probably already knew how to go to the temple to pray. They knew the posture and the words, but when they watched Jesus pray, they saw something different. They wanted to be able to fellowship with the Father like Jesus did. He granted their request with the model prayer.

"When you pray, say, 'Our Father who is in heaven, hallowed be your name. Your kingdom come. Your will be done on earth as it is in heaven....'" Jesus was telling them that they would participate in the expression of the kingdom of God, which had come to earth in him. Remember, the first man was given partnership with God. Now the last Adam was restoring the dignity destroyed by sin. The followers of Jesus would work with God by praying his kingdom into the earth.

Several years ago I wrote a book entitled *Incense and Thunder*. I had been reading the Book of Revelation, which is an apocalyptic treatise. In this kind of literature there is usually a vision and a guide in the vision who explains the symbols. John the apostle had such a vision and saw many symbols needing explanation. One phenomenon he saw was incense rising from earth to heaven. The angel of the Lord mixed the smoke with fire from the altar and flung it back to earth as thunder, lightening, and earthquakes. When this was explained to John, he was told that this is what prayer looks like in heaven. The saints send up their incense and God moves aspects of heaven into earth to give instruction, revelation and transformation.

As we move around trying to manage the garden God has allotted to us, we see things that are contrary to the order of God's kingdom. Our privilege and responsibility is to pray the kingdom order into that situation. As we see the kingdom of God, we pray for it to replace the kingdoms of deception and destruction that currently reign.

Someone may ask, "Does prayer actually change anything? Is it primarily for our benefit, like good therapy? How can God be sovereign and still give us the assignment to pray for changes to happen?" Maybe an illustration from the Old Testament will help. When Moses went up on the mountain to meet with God, the people of Israel began to worship a false god. As Moses met with God about it, God declared that he would wipe them out and start over with Moses. This is what they deserved. It would have been justice and God would have been totally in the right to destroy them, but Moses prayed for God's higher purpose. He knew the nature of God and prayed that God's mercy would trump justice. He reminded God of what God already knew – God had purposed to make Israel his people of witness. And God answered Moses' prayer. Did he change his mind? Yes, but he didn't change his heart. Moses prayed the ultimate order of God, and God answered.

We don't ever have to talk God into being better. We can discover what his kingdom looks like, which will always be better than the one we see with our natural eyes, and pray accordingly.

We have great confidence when we pray according to his will (1 John 5:14). So how do we pray according to his will? We can begin by praying according to the covenant now in effect. We don't live in the old covenant era. We live under the conditions of the new covenant. Often we are encouraged to pray according to the model found in the dedication of the Solomon's Temple:

> *If my people who are called by my name humble themselves, and pray and seek my face and turn from their wicked ways, then I will hear from heaven and will forgive their sin and heal their land*
>
> 2 Chronicles 7:14 (ESV)

Here God is responding to Solomon's earlier prayer. He tells Solomon he will honor the Temple as a place where he will meet with his people. They are in covenant with him, and if they ignore that covenant they will suffer in the land with natural catastrophes. But if they will respond in humble repentance, he will hear them there and heal their land.

Some have tried to transpose that promise to other lands. God was not addressing the USA or any other nation. He was addressing Israel at that time. Of course, the transcendent truth of God's willingness to respond in mercy to his people is always applicable. But if we interpret that promise in light of the cross of Christ and the new covenant he has inaugurated, we will see that the people addressed are followers of Christ, not just Americans, and that the land is the inheritance we have because we are in Christ. The sins we must address are the neglect of the grace found in him and the refusal to embrace the benefits of the new covenant.

We are New Testament Christians and our prayers should reflect that.

Prayer is a priority. Nothing is more important for us than to know God to the fullest degree possible. We have been called to participate in the manifestation of the kingdom of God on earth. God has granted us the privilege of working with him in doing his will. The apostle Paul encouraged believers to "pray without ceasing". Of course, he was not suggesting that they suspend every aspect of life in order to verbally pray all the time. He was emphasizing the need to stay attuned to the realm of ultimate reality so we can pray effectively.

So how would it look to pray the kingdom's coming?

For government, we can pray that God will guide the leaders to make clear and simple laws that will protect the citizens from internal and external oppression, and free them to manage their own lives with opportunity to trade with each other. That is the purpose of government in society.

For the church, we can pray that it will awaken to its societal responsibilities of defining and declaring truth while equipping its members to demonstrate the kingdom of God in every sphere of influence. If it gets distracted from this role, all of society will suffer.

For the home, we can pray that families will model the family of God with mutual submission and clear division of labor, that the members will be nurtured and empowered to discover their destiny in relation to God's purpose.

For individuals, we can pray for unbelievers to have their eyes opened to see the gospel in the face of Jesus Christ (2 Corinthians 4:3-5). We can pray for believers to have eyes opened to see their inheritance in Christ and to walk in it. Both have a "seeing" problem we can address in prayer. Remember, when we pray, God sends lightning and thunder, so they can see and hear the truth that will set them free.

This is a day when God is calling his people to take seriously their privilege in prayer. We are partners with him.

9. The Orphan Finds Mercy

The prophet Hosea received quite an unusual assignment from the Lord. He was to marry a prostitute named Gomer. Even after making a marriage covenant with Hosea, Gomer had children by other men. This was a picture of the nation of Israel at that time. Israel, like Gomer, was in covenant with God but had pursued other lovers. She was hopelessly drawn to idols. The whole book of Hosea is about this idolatrous relationship. God had every right to divorce and banish this false lover. Israel adopted the gods of the surrounding culture, yet tried to keep her own festivals and worship rituals. The results were ritual without relationship and information without transformation.

It sounds a lot like today, doesn't it? Some are boasting of the numbers of churches being built and the numbers of people attending, but the quality of life of the typical church-attendee is no better than that of those who do not attend. There is not much evidence of people having been truly transformed by the power of the gospel. The level of joy in the typical American Christian is very low. Few pagans are attracted to a superior lifestyle enjoyed by a modern American Christian. The American dream is more popular and more motivating than the gospel of the kingdom portrayed in our churches. Many Christians have little hope that they can rid themselves of addictions and perversions.

So, what did God do with Israel? When he had every right to destroy her, he offered her mercy.

*Return, O Israel, to the Lord your God, for you have stumbled because of your iniquity. Take with you words and return to the Lord; say to him, "Take away all iniquity; accept what is good, and we will pay with bulls the vows of our lips. Assyria shall not save us; we will not ride on horses; and we will say no more, 'Our God' to the work of our hands. **In you the orphan finds mercy"** (emphasis mine).*

Hosea 14:1-3 (ESV)

God so wants to restore his people that he invites them to return to him. He even tells them the words to say when they do. Their speech is to conclude and climax with the affirmation: "In you the orphan finds mercy."

He is telling them – and us – that idolatry and adultery have their roots in the orphan spirit. Israel had been called as God's son (see Exodus 4:22). Adam was the first son who was to enjoy God and partner with him in subduing the earth, but Adam and Eve sinned and introduced the orphan perspective to humanity. Before their sin, they had unhindered access to the Father and his provisions. Since their fall, all of mankind has been trying to live from behind the bush of shame. Being cut off from the source of real life, we have sought to satisfy our longings by going after whatever and whoever offered the best deal. Israel had been called to represent God the Father to the world, so God had given her the privileges of sonship. But because at heart she was an orphan, she could only partially trust God. The other enticements from more visible gods would be embraced as well.

One thing is clear for Israel and for us: the quality of life we experience depends on the gods we trust. If we have adequate gods, we will have quality life. If we have poorly performing gods, then life goes into the tank. Of course we know that only the God of the Bible, who is fully revealed in Jesus, is truly adequate, but we still find ourselves trusting lesser gods. Theoretically, we know the right information about God, but functionally we get trapped by the idolatry produced by our orphan-perspective. When asked who our savior is, we quickly respond, "Jesus." But functionally, is that true?

Who saves us from sin? Is it Jesus? What about the effort we exert trying to make sure we have made up for lapses in our behavior by engaging in religious or charitable works? What about the penalty we assess ourselves when we sin? We tend to refuse to enjoy life for fear we are being presumptuous towards God's mercy. Like college football programs facing the NCAA, we penalize ourselves hoping the larger authority will take that into consideration when judgment is meted out.

Who saves us from meaninglessness? Is it Jesus? Isn't it our success at our vocation or family? Don't we spend more time and energy trying to be recognized as successful in our performance before our peers than in rejoicing in the reality that we are sons of God and have meaning in representing him on the earth?

Who saves us from error? Is it Jesus who is the living truth? Too often we rest in the rightly articulated creeds and doctrinal statements that offer safety and identity. What about the joy of walking in relationship with the living truth and ever learning new aspects of his perspective? We get so concerned about absolutes and forget that the absolute truth is living and available to us daily.

Who saves us from poverty? Jesus? Most of us don't really believe this. It is our savings, or our job, or our skill that we rely on. What happened to the son's faith that his father will never forsake him or fail to provide everything needed to accomplish his assignment?

Idols need to be exposed! All of us orphans have them, and God's mercy exposes them. He wants to displace them with himself. Timothy Keller in his book, *Counterfeit Gods*, mentions several ways to identify idols. First, our idle thoughts can be good clues. What do we enjoy thinking about when our thoughts are not required for other duties? In an age where visionaries are championed, there are many who spend every possible moment of imagination in trying to accomplish something new, big and successful. What about seeking and savoring the beauty of Christ and his life? Second, unjustified spending can help us to uncover hidden idols. When we continually go outside a reasonable budget to get something we "just have to have" to make us happy, we are getting close to creating a god. Third, when we are honest about uncontrollable emotions, we are getting serious about displacing false gods. When fear, or lust, or ambition, or anger regularly boil over, it is usually the result of trusting something other than God our Father to meet our needs. Then there is the clincher. When disappointment comes, do we move towards or away from intimacy with God? When we have worked hard for something and even prayed for it, only to have our hopes dashed, it is difficult to maintain a stable level of joy and hope – especially when others who have not been as diligent get the rewards. Orphans are so fragile we cannot endure much of this. We thought we could put God in debt to us by good works or moral living. We had thus created a false god who cannot perform what we demand for our pleasure. Only when we truly see God the Father as our source and trust him completely will our inadequate gods disappear.

One thing we can be sure of (and it is very good news): God loves orphans. Notice that he was willing to come to his son, Israel, who was neck deep in idolatry and restore the relationship.

(Hosea, reflecting God's nature, searched for Gomer and bought her back to be his wife after her adultery.)

One of the Old Testament characters who illustrates this dynamic is Jacob. He was the second-born twin brother of Esau. His life was about striving. He came out of the womb holding the heel of his brother. His father preferred Esau and so cemented Jacob's orphan mind-set. He longed for the father's blessing so much that he schemed to get it. Tricking his father and defrauding his brother, he got the official blessing, but it did not satisfy. He was a son who thought and acted like the ultimate orphan.

Running from Esau, he went to a new area and saw Rachel. He had to have her and spent some years scheming with her father for her. But even Rachael couldn't satisfy Jacob's needs. As he ran from Esau (actually Esau was coming to reconcile, but the orphan Jacob interpreted everything through fear and thought Esau was coming to kill him), he had a night to spend alone before the great encounter with Esau. That night he wrestled with God. God actually came to this pitiful orphan schemer, full of fear and manipulation, and wrestled with him. We know that God doesn't have to wrestle with humans. He could have evaporated Jacob with his breath, but he gave the striver a chance to see the end of his striving. In the match, the angel touched his thigh and he was disabled from striving against the angel. Before dawn, as the angel was leaving, Jacob would not let him go "until you bless me."

What a cry! He had lived his whole life wanting to be blessed. He had striven, cheated, lied, and connived. Now, when he can fight no more, he holds on for a blessing. It is mercy when God brings us to the end of our striving so we can find victory in our weakness. No longer do we have to pretend to be strong. We don't have to defend our position or identity. We need not boast of our sonship. We can rest in it.

One day in Jacob's future, there would be another who demonstrated that in God's economy you win when you are weak. He was the eternal Son, but he became a servant to Israel and to mankind. He became a sacrifice for sin. He defeated every enemy of mankind and started a new creation of people whose names and identities were changed. He made it possible for all orphans to find mercy in him. He doesn't just change our names in the book; he changes our status with God, and he gives us the Spirit of sonship, energizing us to enjoy God as Father and live in vital fellowship with him.

But how do we actually access this? What is our responsibility now? The New Testament doesn't leave us in the dark. Much of the latter part of the New Testament encourages us to intentionally set our minds on the truth of what Jesus has done to reconcile us to God as Father. Here is one of the texts:

> *If then you have been raised with Christ, seek the things that are above, where Christ is, seated at the right hand of God. Set your minds on things that are above, not on things that are on earth. For you have died, and your life is hidden with Christ in God.*
>
> Colossians 3:1-3 (ESV)

Idols are not torn down, they are displaced by the true God. When we are in relationship with him we won't need substitutes. Idols are evidence of an orphan mentality. When the orphan finds mercy and discovers that God is his Father, he will have no need of false security and significance.

10. Crossing Over and Carrying On

God has always been intent on having his people enjoy the inheritance he gave them. In the Old Testament he used physical and natural shadows to depict the spiritual and ultimate reality he had in mind for his final people on earth. The story of Joshua is a type of the ultimate Savior who would lead the people into the land of fulfilled promise so that they could embrace their inheritance from the Father.

In the first chapter of the Old Testament book of Joshua, God defines the inheritance for Joshua specifically and generously. He then promises to be with Joshua personally to defend and provide. He will just as surely support Joshua as he supported Moses. A transition in history has occurred, for Moses is dead and a new day has arrived. This pointed to another day in their future when the era of the Law (Moses) would give way to the era of the new covenant.

> *"For the law was given through Moses; grace and truth came through Jesus Christ."*
> John 1:17 (ESV).

Then God commanded Joshua to be courageous as he embarked on this journey of possessing the inheritance. He would need courage to believe God when all circumstances were contrary. And then God told him how to maintain that courage. He was to meditate on the words that God had given so that he could do them.

This Book of the Law shall not depart from your mouth,
but you shall meditate on it day and night, so that you
may be careful to do according to all that is written in it.
For then you will make your way prosperous, and then
you will have good success.

Joshua 1:8 (ESV)

Understanding that this event in history points toward a greater and fuller inheritance, we can use it to help us embrace the land of promise we have received.

What is our inheritance?

We live in the era of the new covenant. Jesus is both our Joshua and our inheritance. We are no longer looking for real estate since we have been given a person who is our identity, provision and protection. Eternal life is the very life that Jesus lived on earth and now lives in heaven. We are the people of God designed to enjoy him and demonstrate his life here and forever.

In him we have obtained an inheritance, having been
predestined according to the purpose of him who works
all things according to the counsel of his will, so that we
who were the first to hope in Christ might be to the praise
of his glory.

Ephesians 1:11-12 (ESV)

The children of Israel under Joshua were a type of the ultimate people under Jesus who would be able to fulfill the assignment of being representatives of God on the earth.

But you are a chosen race, a royal priesthood, a holy na-
tion, a people for his own possession, that you may pro-
claim the excellencies of him who called you out of
darkness into his marvelous light.

1 Peter 2:9 (ESV)

Our inheritance includes the Spirit who raised Jesus from the grave and now works in us to do God's will. He gifts us and empowers us to know and express the life of the resurrected Lord. And then there is the partnership arrangement God has made with us. We are his instruments of redemption until everything marred by sin is restored to God's intentions.

What did the inheritance look like to the New Testament audience?

We know that for Joshua's generation the inheritance was about taking land and fighting nations. But after Jesus had come to fulfill the shadows with the substance of ultimate truth, how did the early disciples see the inheritance? Pentecost was a dramatic demonstration that a new era had arrived. Before it, the temple had been the center of religious activity for God's people. Now the disciples were being made living temples of the Holy Spirit. Old Testament prophecies were being fulfilled. They experienced miraculous signs that vindicated them as God's people. They lived with a consciousness of God's presence and demonstrated they were in touch with a reality beyond the physical.

Like Joshua, the disciples faced battles. They did not fight flesh and blood with swords and spears; however, they were fighting the battles of the real war.

For though we walk in the flesh, we are not waging war according to the flesh. For the weapons of our warfare are not of the flesh but have divine power to destroy strongholds. We destroy arguments and every lofty opinion raised against the knowledge of God...
                                                    2 Corinthians 10:3-5 (ESV)

They suffered severe persecution from the Jews who would not recognize Jesus as the truth. They were also persecuted by secular powers that were threatened by people who submitted to a Lord more powerful than Caesar. To win this war they had to walk in truth. Deception was the enemy. They also exhibited hope in a fuller salvation than they were experiencing at the time. They knew inheritance had dawned, but they were sure there was more to be embraced. They believed that their enemies would be judged, and they were.

In 70 AD, the city of Jerusalem, along with its temple, was destroyed. The Jewish system was finished. Christianity would no longer be viewed as a sect of Judaism. It was launched as the kingdom of God invading the earth. Later on, the secular authorities of Rome had their day. Rome was the most secure empire the world had known. However, Rome was destroyed, while the people of God increased. But even that was not the final hope.

They looked forward to the judgment of all things and the resurrection of the body. They had seen Jesus after the resurrection and knew that one day they too would have such a body. Since this hope was firmly in their hearts, they were courageous. Not even death could threaten them. They would live forever with Christ, and death held no fear. They were consumed with proclaiming to the ends of the earth this gospel that had transformed them. They knew it would change people and that changed people would change societies. They believed they had been given the mandate to subdue creation by making disciples of Jesus Christ, and they rejoiced in every opportunity to testify of him.

What does the inheritance look like to us?

We weren't present at the original Pentecost, but we continue to live with its benefits. We are indwelt by the Holy Spirit and are empowered to demonstrate the life of God's kingdom on earth. We have a written record of how the first century disciples interpreted their inheritance, and so we have a model to follow. The Gospels reveal Jesus as the Seed of Abraham, the Son of God, the Son of Man, and the Eternal Word. The Acts of The Apostles demonstrate what life looks like when people take their inheritance seriously. The Epistles reveal how to apply the truth Jesus imparted. The Revelation sums up the whole Bible and exalts Jesus as the Joshua who faithfully and successfully leads his people into the ultimate victory over every enemy.

The events of 70 AD and the fall of Rome are behind us. We can now see that for which the New Testament disciples hoped. We have confidence that all opposing powers and ideologies will fall in due time. The kingdom that was inaugurated by Jesus will not be thwarted by any power, religious or secular. Communism, Marxism, Islam, Post-modernism, and all other "isms" will fall under the ever-penetrating power of the gospel of the kingdom of God.

We look for the completion of the new heavens and the new earth. Jesus began the new creation with his resurrection, and it continues to develop as truth displaces error. The creation is in the groaning stage now but one day will be restored to the original design. There will be a judgment of all things when every wrong will be made right. There will be a resurrection of the body and God's creation will eternally shout the praises of him who redeems completely. All creation will respond to the King in the way it was designed — full submission and eternal praise.

How do we claim it?

This inheritance is already ours! It has been transferred to us by Jesus' mediation. The new covenant is in effect now. Just like the land of Promise was given to the Israelites, yet they still had to occupy it, so we have to embrace what has been given to us as the people of God's covenant.

It is by believing! The battles we fight are against the attacks on grace. The big temptation is to believe we have to fight to gain our inheritance. The fight is to believe we have been GIVEN the inheritance. It is not a reward for good behavior. It is a gift to be opened.

Probably the clearest instruction regarding claiming the new covenant inheritance is found in Ephesians 4:17-32. Paul makes a clear distinction between the way unbelievers (Gentiles) think and the way the followers of Jesus think. Unbelievers are thinking in futility regarding the gospel, while Christians are taught by Jesus himself.

Now this I say and testify in the Lord, that you must no longer walk as the Gentiles do, in the futility of their minds. They are darkened in their understanding, alienated from the life of God because of the ignorance that is in them, due to their hardness of heart. They have become callous and have given themselves up to sensuality, greedy to practice every kind of impurity. But that is not the way you learned Christl— assuming that you have heard about him and were taught in him, as the truth is in Jesus, to put off your old self, which belongs to your former manner of life and is corrupt through deceitful desires, and to be renewed in the spirit of your minds, and to put on the new self, created after the likeness of God in true righteousness and holiness.
Ephesians 4:17-24 (ESV)

Paul uses the metaphor of changing clothes. The old clothes are the life we live when we believe the deceptions of ignorance about God. The new clothes are the life we live when we believe the truth. There are three aspects to the action. We are first to **PUT OFF the old**. This means we are to recognize this behavior as unacceptable. It cannot be tolerated, rationalized, or justified but must be identified as wrong and destructive. Then we are to be **RENEWED in the spirit of the mind**. This is the crucial choice. We must adopt a new way of viewing reality. Only those who have the Spirit of God can see accurately in the Spirit. They evaluate everything differently now that they believe they are sons of God rather than the orphans of Adam's race. Now, they can **PUT ON the new behavior**. As they act according to what God says is true, he will enable them to act in ways that heretofore were impossible for them. They had been ignorant and unable to respond. Now they can see; they have been energized by the indwelling Spirit of Christ. This process must be repeated many times before it becomes habitual.

Thankfully Paul gives some examples of how this works. He takes up the issue of lying. It must be named for what it is: falsehood. It is wrong and unacceptable. Now there must be a renewed perspective: "We are members one of another." This makes lying nonsensical. Why would one member of your body lie to another member? It would be counterproductive. Since our new purpose is to encourage every member of the body, we look for ways to speak the truth. Truth will liberate them and enable them to succeed in the kingdom of God. Because our purpose has changed, our behavior will change. We choose to speak the truth. It is more than just choosing not to lie. It is proactive. We know the truth about them and we put it into words. We remind them of

God's grace towards them. This truth speaking displaces the lying that was part of the old perspective.

Paul also addresses anger. It is not always wrong to be angry. Anger is often the result of perceived injustice. However it is unacceptable to seethe in anger. It gives the devil an opportunity to pervert thinking and exalt bitterness. Since we know the danger, we can choose to deal with it immediately ("before the sun goes down"). If there is an injustice, we either address it or forgive it. If it is only perceived, we correct the perception.

Paul addresses stealing as well. The orphan steals because he believes he doesn't have enough to provide for his needs. The son has everything he needs and works for the purpose of having some to give to those who don't have enough. This work ethic will produce good work and generosity. Stealing has no place in a worldview like this.

Paul goes on to apply this three-fold dynamic to several other issues. He is telling us that we have new clothes. This is not an instruction manual for us to follow so that we can qualify for grace and avoid punishment. It is a description of what is in our closet, having been put there by our Father for our enjoyment and success.

Let us, like Joshua, be courageous in embracing the inheritance we have been given. The Lord told him that a key to his success was meditating on the Law. We can learn from him. We must intentionally meditate on the truth revealed in the full revelation of the Law – Jesus the Christ and our Lord. If we are serious about actually living as sons, we will recognize that our minds are still occupied with many perceptions we adopted when we were thinking like spiritual orphans. We have the privilege of renewing the mind and choosing to live by a new perspective. It will be worth the time and energy spent in absorbing the word of God. A few devotional moments and some visits to the local church probably won't get the job done. Serious sons, intent on investigating the whole inheritance, will find ways to meditate on the truth of grace found in the scriptures as illumined by the Spirit. There is yet a lot to be discovered and embraced. Let's not waste time.

11. Learning to Live Loved

It is a shame that the concept of eternal life has been so abused. For most Christians it brings up thoughts of heaven or of life after death. When Jesus spoke of it, he was describing the very relationship he enjoyed with the Father (John 17:3). It is far more than a ticket to heaven. It is the daily dynamic of being conscious of another's presence and perspective. It is living with an awareness of another's opinion of me.

In the last discourse with his disciples, Jesus framed eternal life in terms of God's greatest commandment. He states that he is giving them a new commandment and this alone is remarkable. Jesus is claiming the authority to alter the Great Commandment God had given in previous days. But what is new about it? The Great Commandment says we are to love God with everything we have and to love our neighbor as ourselves. The new commandment says we are to love as Jesus loves us.

We should note that the commandment is first about love, not behavioral modification. Our history proves we can't even maintain the love required by the previous commandment. We have spurts and sputters in our attempts to love God with our whole heart. Our love apparatus is bent. We invariably love ourselves but with a crooked kind of love. So when we try to love others we love them with the same crooked love. We need someone whose ability to love has not been perverted by self-obsession.

Jesus loved perfectly, and his love transformed a bunch of ordinary selfish men. How did he love like that? He was loved and he knew it. When he and the disciples had met for that final Passover meal, he noticed that no one had washed their feet. So he arose and adopted the role of the menial servant. John explains that he could do that because he knew that the Father had given him all things, and that he had come from God and was going back to God. In other words, he knew that God the Father loved him unconditionally, thus he could love his imperfect and insensitive disciples until the end.

When Jesus prayed for his disciples he asked that they might enjoy the same love from the Father he experienced:

> *I made known to them your name, and I will continue to make it known, that the love with which you have loved me may be in them, and I in them.*
>
> John 17:26 (ESV).

As we believe in Jesus as our life, we too can expect to love the way he loves. It is part of the inheritance we have been given as sons of God. Just think of it: living with total confidence that regardless of how we are perceived by others, we are assured of acceptance and full support from our Father. What kind of confidence would that allow?

You may have heard the statement: "I am not loved because I am valuable; I am valuable because I am loved." It expresses the difference in the way the world's system defines us and the way the kingdom of God defines us. Sadly, we most often operate by the world's definition of love. When we conclude we are loved only as we prove ourselves valuable, we become slaves of performance. We tend to turn every activity into a competition to prove ourselves. Regardless of our insistence that it doesn't matter what others think, we all need to feel valued. Being valued for service rendered and being loved are not the same, but we are usually willing to redefine love in those terms. Crowds scream, "We love you!" to performers on stage. They don't really. They don't even know the performer. They value them for their skills or talents, but it is not the kind of love you can build life upon. Being loved is better than being valued for services given. This is what Jesus offers to his people.

Recently there were some new inductees into the National Football League's Hall of Fame. One of the inductees was Jerry Rice, probably the best receiver ever. In his speech he admitted to achieving his lofty goals in response to fear of failure. He said that he was pushed by the thought of not living up to the expectations of family, friends, and coaches. He also confessed that he had never stopped to enjoy the journey. He was too possessed with the desire to succeed to even enjoy the game and its benefits. At the end of his speech, he walked around the podium and asked the audience for the privilege of taking a breath and enjoying the moment. It lasted less than 10 seconds. I was saddened by the thought that one of the most admired and respected football players of all time had traded more than twenty years of hard work for ten seconds of enjoyment. Now that he can't perform and prove his value, will he know he is loved? Will a bust in the Hall of Fame suffice for a testimony of his value? Will those who don't know his reputation as a Hall of Famer see any reason to love him?

There is no earthly Hall of Fame for the rest of us. There is no bust in Canton to prove we are valuable. We will have to judge our value some other way, and there are options. We can compare our performance with others for relative value, or we can live in denial about the need to be valued, or we can find our value in being loved by God.

Could Jerry Rice have been as great a player if he was not driven by fear? Well, of course. If we could be better motivated by fear than by love, Jesus would have left us in our fears. Love always propels us higher than fear can drive us. Being loved by Him is the highest possible testimony of our value.

Who does Jesus love? The most obvious answer is: everyone. I am referring to which person in an individual does he love. We all have at least three personas we maintain. First we have the **presentable** me. That is the "me" of actions, reputations, behavior, and resumes. I work to refine this social me. He is the one that others see first and foremost. I want him to look refined and acceptable. Second, there is the **private** me. That is the "me" of thoughts and feelings. Only those close enough to observe me under pressure, or those trusted enough to allow me to be vulnerable, would know this person. The third persona is the **perverted** me. That is the "me" of shame. He is the one I keep caged, because he is capable of barbaric thoughts and deeds. No one can really know him and still feel safe. Only God knows him, and we sure hope he keeps his mouth shut. If others ever see him they will run away. Yet this is the person Jesus loves! The other two are trying to prove themselves worthy of love, while this one knows he can never measure up.

It is to this caged monster that Jesus came in his death and resurrection. He approached the cell wearing the barbaric, twisted, and shameful deeds, and died to put them away forever. The prisoner can now step out. Not only is he not punished for his perversion; he is valued as a son of God. He is treated with the same dignity as the Son who took his place. He can breathe now. He can risk exposure. He is covered by a love that declares him acceptable.

Paul, the apostle to the church at Corinth, talks about this "inner me".

> *For this reason I bow my knees before the Father, from whom every family in heaven and on earth is named, that according to the riches of his glory he may grant you to be strengthened with power through his Spirit in your **inner being**, so that Christ may dwell in your hearts through faith—that you, being rooted and grounded in love, may have strength to comprehend with all the saints what is the breadth and length and height and depth, and to know the love of Christ that surpasses knowledge, that you may be filled with all the fullness of God (emphasis mine).*
>
> Ephesians 3:14-19 (ESV)

Paul's prayer reveals his understanding that we change from the inner person and that we change when we embrace being loved.

It is interesting to note that John mentions the saga of Peter immediately after Jesus tells of the new commandment. Peter is sure he is able to go wherever Jesus goes. He is sure he can perform better than all the other disciples. He wants desperately to be worthy of Christ's approval. He has been pushed his whole life to prove his value. He has never let any audience doubt that he had gifts, skills, and personality that made him valuable. He has always been out front. But now it was time for him to confront the caged man inside. There was a lurking coward inside the man who looked so brave. There was a sniveling, fearful little boy trying to convince himself and others that he was worthy of being valued.

We all know the story of how he stood beside a fire to warm himself on that chilly night. He was exposed by a question from a little girl. Before sunrise he had denied the Lord three times. The gig was up! The one who had professed his love above his fellows was an embarrassment. He abandoned his hope and went fishing, back to the old life before Jesus invited him to follow. He was dismissing the prophecy that Jesus had spoken over him, "You are a rock. . .." He was discounting the revelation he had received about Jesus being the Christ. He was facing reality and it wasn't pretty. The man that defined him was the perverted one. He might as well settle for being a good fisherman while other more valuable people got to do the important things.

In the meantime, Jesus goes to the cross, descends to the lower parts, confronts the caged man inside Peter (and the rest of us), opens the cell door and trades places with the perverted man. After his resurrection he finds Peter to reveal to him the good news. Peter and the boys are fishing when they see Jesus on the shore cooking breakfast. Peter runs ahead again straight to Jesus who will confront the deepest level of Peter's existence: "Do you love me?"

Notice that Jesus did not deal with the behavioral aspects of Peter's failure. It was not the "presentable man" that concerned him. He did not address the emotional aspects of Peter's failure. He was not dealing with the childhood scars that had caused Peter to feel pressured to perform. He went straight to the love-apparatus. Only love changes the inner man. Peter mumbled as honest an answer as he could muster, "I am fond of you." Then Jesus springs it on him: "Feed my sheep!" Jesus wouldn't hand that job off to someone who didn't or couldn't love his sheep. Jesus is the Good Shepherd and is vitally concerned with his sheep. Anyone who represents him as a shepherd must be like him. Jesus was telling Peter that he qualified. He was valuable, not because he had proven it, but because Jesus had placed value in him.

Peter would spend the rest of his life learning how to embrace this love. He would have to believe the words of Jesus above all feelings, circumstances, and opinions of others. I think he finally got it. He died a martyr after preaching the Pentecostal sermon, writing some of the New Testament and shepherding Jesus' sheep for a number of years. He is valuable to all subsequent believers for the services he has provided for us. He was valuable to Jesus because Jesus loved him.

So how do we learn to live loved?

I suggest a three-pronged approach. **First, we embrace the Father's discipline (Hebrews 12).** He is not punishing his sons when tough times occur. He is exposing them to their own inability so he can reveal his ability in them. He led Israel through the wilderness so he could reveal his Fatherly love to them. He fed them with manna and fought through them to win victories over much larger armies. He taught them to live by his word rather than what appeared to be true. He left enemies in the land to teach them how to fight by faith and not just by sword. Often they interpreted their trials as evidence that God had forsaken them, but each obstacle was an expression of his love and determination to get them to their inheritance.

Second, we choose to believe the words of Jesus and trust the efficacy of his work. With so many voices interpreting reality to us, we cannot afford to neglect his words to us. He is the final and complete Word of God to creation. He alone has the right to define truth, so his word must become the final conclusion on every matter. This does not mean that we limit our reading of the New Testament to the Gospels. His word includes the remainder of the Scriptures that help us understand what his words in the Gospels mean.

Third, we expect the Spirit of God to work in us what Jesus has said to us. He works in the inner man to reveal our adoption as sons. He mysteriously transforms us as we trust. Paul mentioned that the love of Christ is "beyond knowledge", past our understanding. It works with the same kind of miraculous energy as a seed when it germinates, but even greater. As we expect the Spirit to make real our sonship, we anticipate the possible responses we can have now that we see things differently. We can meditate on how this will affect the way we view our friends, our finances, the pressures of work, possible surprises, and difficult circumstances. We can visualize how we might approach these now that we believe we are sons of God who are loved with the same love as the Father loves the Son. Then when the time arrives, we have already practiced it in our mind. I think this must be included in what Paul meant when he said to "put on the new man." When we are plunked down in the middle of a crisis, we don't need to have to think new thoughts. If we haven't put on the new man, we probably will revert to the default mode of thinking like an orphan or the unloved caged man. It is a process of rejecting the old, renewing the way we think, and reviewing the way these new thoughts will change the way we act.

12. All Signs Point to Him

The gospel of John is all about the eternal life that Jesus demonstrated while on earth. John builds his story around some miraculous signs that Jesus performed. These signs point toward the opportunity to believe in Jesus as the Christ, the Son of God, and to have the same life he enjoys with the Father (see John 20:30-31).

Jesus' first sign was at Cana of Galilee where he turned several pots of water into wine. This sign demonstrated his role as the fulfillment of previous shadows. Moses had turned the river into blood. Jesus turns water into wine. Water pots had been for purification in the Old Testament system, but Jesus offers cleansing through his blood and life in the Spirit. Though he is a guest, he performs the duties of the bridegroom. He does all of this in the context of a wedding pointing to the intimate relationship he is providing for his followers.

Then, Jesus went to Jerusalem for the feast and performed some miraculous works there. When he came back, people wanted to see some more miraculous works. They liked the made-to-order miracles where Jesus served to meet their demands.

So when he came to Galilee, the Galileans welcomed him, having seen all that he had done in Jerusalem at the feast. For they too had gone to the feast.
So he came again to Cana in Galilee, where he had made the water wine. And at Capernaum there was an official whose son was ill. When this man heard that Jesus had

come from Judea to Galilee, he went to him and asked him to come down and heal his son, for he was at the point of death. So Jesus said to him, "Unless you see signs and wonders you will not believe." The official said to him, "Sir, come down before my child dies." Jesus said to him, "Go; your son will live." The man believed the word that Jesus spoke to him and went on his way.

John 4:45-50 (ESV)

The rest of the story tells how the man went on his journey back home. The next day he is met by servants who told him that the boy was healed at the seventh hour of the previous day – the exact time Jesus spoke the word to the father.

We can easily make application for our culture. Those people were enamored with the miraculous power Jesus displayed and they could see how to leverage that for their own benefits. They could get Jesus to enhance their already established values and goals. They liked the signs, they just didn't know to what they pointed. Jesus was offering them life, and they were content to have some excitement and assistance.

A culture's hope is whatever it proclaims life is all about. America's hope is the good life as defined by gaining wealth and maintaining or restoring health. We like better jobs, bigger houses, closer parking spaces and superior entertainment. In our focus on comfort and convenience we have nurtured ourselves into lazy bodies and sloppy minds.

Recently I saw a commercial touting a program for college students that guaranteed to wake them for their classes. It seems bad grades are a result of grown young adults being unable to respond to an alarm clock and get to class. What's next? A program that takes them to the bathroom?

In the church realm we have refused to think through biblical theology and have instead substituted cute quips and clichés for our spiritual foundations. We confess "once saved always saved", trying to explain the wonderful mystery in God's sovereign choices and man's responsibility. We quip that "a good father would never permit his children to be sick or hurt", when in fact God leads his children into the wilderness to experience the end of their own strength in order to trust his. "Jesus is perfect theology," says the healing preacher, and then he goes on to explain that we should model our healing ministry after Jesus. And since there is no record of anyone coming to him in faith failing to be healed, we should strive for similar results. Of course, Jesus is perfect theology, but the gospels are not the last books in the New Testament. The early disciples lived out what Jesus had taught, leaving us a record of their experiences and the conclusions they reached as together they were led by the Spirit.

The big thoughts of God's revelation are not easily expressed in modern slogans designed to brand and market the message. Big thoughts require big thinking and that usually requires more than a phrase. The early church spent years (and pages) in prayer and discussion to clarify theological issues for their time. We could benefit from their conclusions as well as their approach.

When the fleshly mindset defines reality, God's word is interpreted primarily to alleviate our discomfort. We conclude that Jesus lives to make our American dream come true. We figure we have a right to expect him to do whatever is necessary to make the lifestyle we have chosen better. So Jesus is valued because of his assistance in gaining wealth and restoring health.

We live in the era of the Spirit. Since Jesus ascended to the right hand of the Father, we have been given the Holy Spirit, who makes Christ's work and word real to us. Jesus still speaks his word to us, and we have the privilege of believing him. When that happens, the Word becomes flesh again in our situations. We are not yet living in the eternal state where all faith has become sight, but we do live in the era when we can embrace the word of Christ and enjoy the life he has given.

There is a divine process in this era. The apostle Paul explains it in Romans 10:5-17. The act of faith culminates in people calling on the name of the Lord. This means more than just a desperate call to anyone who might be listening. It is recognition that Jesus has been made Lord of all things and that we are putting our trust in his ability and willingness to exert that lordship in our behalf. But how can they call on someone they don't trust? So trust must precede our calling. But how can they trust in someone they have not heard? They can't just create their own designer god and then expect him to act on their behalf. Someone must proclaim the true nature of the Lord. But who can do that? Only those who are sent by God to clearly explain the "word of Christ." But what is the word of Christ? It is the message that Jesus is the one expected in all Old Testament promises and predictions. He is the fulfillment of Israel's hope. He is the full explanation of the Son of God, the Son of Man, the Son of Abraham, and the Son of David. It is the proclamation of this message that arouses faith in the hearer.

In our effort to make disciples of Jesus we have tried many approaches but have often overlooked the non-negotiable essential. Some have featured a mentor-centered approach, which often bends toward control. However, unhealthy dependence on the mentor produces weak disciples. Others have tried content-centered discipleship, which usually bends toward isolation and individualism. Still others focus on the program-centered approach, where success is determined by faithfulness in attendance. Lately the relationship-centered approach has been in vogue. That can bend toward cliques where we place boundaries around our fellowship.

Truthfully, there is a need for a balance of all the above with the "word of Christ" kept at the center. Whatever else we do, we must elevate the privilege of each believer to hear the word of Christ in his or her own life. We, as partners with God, can assist in their hearing, but we are not the origin of the word. We must not rely on anything less than the proclaimed, heard, and believed word of Christ.

As we get back to the sign in John, we see that the miracle pointed to the word of Christ dominating the event. The official was rebuked as a member of a society that wanted more signs. He walked through the rebuke and took what Jesus offered. Jesus didn't offer to go with him personally as requested, but he gave his word. The man took the word, and when he heard that his son was healed, he believed in Jesus the person and experienced the life to which the sign had pointed.

Jesus has given us his word, contained in the New Covenant. His whole character is behind it. He will not fail to produce what he has promised, so we don't really need so many more signs. We can follow the signs already given to the life he has offered, and then we can become his instruments of making the word flesh in our circumstances.

People who want more signs will never be satisfied. Yet those who find the promise of life will be totally satisfied. They will experience the joy Jesus has as he relates to the Father as the Son. God did not stop speaking after Pentecost, and he speaks daily to his children as the Holy Spirit makes the word of Christ relevant to us. There is so much we have not yet discovered in Christ. We will spend eternity in the discovery, and we can get started now. There will be miracles – that is just what happens when the kingdom of God interacts with the forces of this world. But the miracles are not the issue. Life is!

13. The Only Worthy Goal

What is the main goal of life? To go to heaven? To be successful in business? To be a better person each day? To do something useful for mankind? To be holy? To be famous? To enjoy life? These are some of the goals that motivate people. I wonder, are they worthy of the energy spent trying to reach them? Are they satisfying when reached?

Actually the life God grants to those who believe in him has a goal.

And this is eternal life, that they know you the only true God, and Jesus Christ whom you have sent.

John 17:3 (ESV)

...these things I speak in the world, that they may have my joy fulfilled in themselves.

John 17:13 (ESV)

What could be greater than knowing God through Jesus Christ? Well, obviously many people think there are better goals. Their time and resources are used up trying to reach less worthy goals. The sense of failure many of us feel is not the recognition that we know God insufficiently, but rather disappointment in not having reached one of our other goals. We fail to identify lack of joy as related to knowing God. It seems we are content to be introduced to him, but never to discover the treasure in knowing him.

Being fallen in Adam, we are predisposed to satisfy ourselves and use everything in our path to do so. Jesus dealt with this as he

95

sought to reveal the true nature of the Father to those who were following him. John's Gospel records seven signs that point to the true nature of God revealed through Jesus the Son. Let's focus on two that particularly show the tendency of his followers to use him to reach their own goals. They want Jesus for the purpose of gaining rescue or provision. However, Jesus wants to show them that he uses rescue and provision to get them to him.

The first sign is the great miracle of Jesus feeding the five thousand. The people stayed so long listening to Jesus they could not make it back home without food. When Moses had been the leader of God's people, manna fell from heaven and fed them, and this sign demonstrates that Jesus is greater than Moses. This time around Jesus not only provides bread for the stomach, he is the bread that satisfies the whole person. After everyone had eaten as much as he or she wanted, the disciples gathered 12 baskets full of leftovers. It was evident that God has plenty in his cupboard. Everyone was full of food and impressed with this miracle, but they missed the sign.

Then the disciples went down to the sea in order to sail to the other side. About half-way across (about 3½ miles out) they encounter a torrential storm. It was terrifying; they could live or die. Fear crawled into the boat. Then when things seemed as bad as they could get, they saw a "ghost" walking over the water. Fear mounted, then the "ghost" spoke. It was Jesus. As soon as he gets into the boat, they are at their destination (John 6:21). The sign is telling us: "Jesus is the destination." When he gets into the boat you are already where you were going.

The next day the crowds discovered where Jesus and his disciples were and began asking for more miracles. Jesus told them that, while they were eager for miracles, they were missing the signs. The signs were pointing to Jesus as the bread of life and the goal of every trip. They just wanted more bread. They wanted to revel in the supernatural events providing for them.

The crowds are typical of all of us. We too want to use Jesus for our provisions, while he wants to use provisions to get us to know him. For instance, we tend to use the Scriptures to find formulas that will enhance our self-centered goals. We find principles of success in business, steps to happier marriages, methods for healing and health, and keys to financial prosperity. We are even tempted to use the gifts of the Spirit to enhance our standing and prop up our lagging confidence. While we distance ourselves from the extreme "prosperity gospel" so glaringly embarrassing on display via TV and other media, we embrace "prosperity-light" in our insistence to bend everything to our own goals of personal security and significance.

"I want to be better." It sounds so honorable to declare that our goal is to be better. Of course, wouldn't "better" be nicer than the way we are now? Think of what that says: It is about us. The standard of success is our status. We are still focused on us and how we feel about ourselves. Wouldn't we feel better about ourselves if we were improving? We would not have as much self-confidence if we were remaining the same. And, what does better look like? Is it a bigger house? A newer car? A better paying job? Less worry? More smiles? Is the goal simply to find a way to "like yourself?"

This unworthy goal leads to embracing a syncretistic religious posture. If the goal is to improve in certain areas so that we are more at peace with ourselves and our surroundings, then many religions offer solutions. Thus the tendency is to group all religions together and eliminate their controversial aspects in an attempt to find a common denominator all can support. "Let's just all get together and work to get better. It doesn't matter how you get there. Just be sincere in your efforts, and we will all find a unity in improvement."

"I'm not going to settle for getting better; I want to be transformed." That is a higher goal. It admits our problem is deeper than we can fix alone. But even transformation is too low; it is still about us. Maybe I have recognized I can't break the chains of addiction and perversion. I am tired of being a slave to a master that continues to disappoint me. I want to be free. But when I am free from those chains, have I embraced life? If I am free to continue living for myself, I am still in big trouble. The disappointment of false freedom can make us vulnerable to those selling techniques and mental exercises for the ultimate answer.

"I just want to be useful." That sounds good. But is being useful simply meeting a need to be valuable so I can merit love? Is the usefulness primarily for my self worth or the benefit of God's purpose?

"I am working to be holy." Certainly holiness is a great reality. However, when it is the primary goal, it will turn into Pharisee-like behavior. We move from being bad to being better to being "better than." We inevitably define holiness in terms of do's and don't's relating to religious behavior, and those who haven't been trained in our definitions of proper religious behavior are considered less than.

So, what is a worthy goal? It has already been given. The Scriptures reveal a Father who delights in his Son, and a Son who delights in his Father. If God the Father could spend eons before creation being delighted in his Son, then he might satisfy us as well. If Jesus could live in the midst of the turmoil of earth being delighted in the Father, then maybe we could, too. God is not our assistant in helping us do our stuff better. Knowing him is the goal that makes all the others work.

Can you imagine being so consumed with his delight that you were not even conscious of your own status? Do you think it might make you a better person in the process of getting your focus above your own needs? Do you think transformation might take place when the lesser gods that promise delight are replaced with the God who more than fulfills our every desire?

Jesus revealed himself so that "his joy might be ours." What is his joy? He delights in honoring the Father, in promoting the Father, and in doing the will of the Father. His joy was the same as the Father's joy. The Father's joy is delighting in his Son. He delights in making his Son the single hero of the universe, in granting his Son the authority to bring heaven to earth. If his joy is to become ours, it means that we delight in something beyond ourselves and our needs.

Throughout history some men and women have determined to reach for the ultimate goal. They found ways to know him more and decided that nothing was worthy of standing in the way of this privilege. As others watched them they noticed particular practices. They valued the "Word of Christ" so highly that they went to great lengths to interpret it, apply it, and ingest it into their very being. Time and schedules had to yield to their pursuits of eating the bread found in the Scriptures. They were not content for popes and pretenders to feed them with milk. They wanted to meet Christ in the Scriptures and would not settle for scattered insights. This became known as a discipline. But the discipline was not the goal, knowing God as Father and Jesus his Son was the goal. Studying and believing the Scriptures was simply the means.

They didn't stop with reading it with understanding. They recognized that the word was so important they should memorize it. Their minds were filled with the thoughts of God through this exercise. They knew that many ideas and concepts came into their minds through the day. They wanted their minds programmed by the truth. They committed to memory large portions of scripture. It wasn't their goal. It was the means to their goal of knowing and delighting in the Father and his Son.

They also spent time meditating on the word of Christ. Since they had it in their storehouse of thoughts, they could use down time in the valuable exercise of rethinking and ruminating on the words inspired by God for the delight of his people. God had told Joshua that his success as a leader of Israel in the Promised Land would be dependent on meditating on the words of God.

> *This Book of the Law shall not depart from your mouth,*
> *but you shall meditate on it day and night, so that you*
> *may be careful to do according to all that is written in it.*
> *For then you will make your way prosperous, and then*
> *you will have good success.*
> Joshua 1:8 (ESV)

The first Psalm declares that meditation on God's words will make a difference in the life of any person (Psalm 1:1-3). Again, the goal is not to see how good at meditating we can become. It is a means to the goal of knowing the delights of God.

It is the same with practices of fasting, silence and solitude. These are not religious currency that we can use to get God's blessings. They are the natural means to employ when our goal is to avoid distraction in order to hear and digest the beauty and delights of God our Father.

For us pragmatists, it seems too mystical to speak of pursuing God and delighting in him, but that is the joy of the journey.

When God placed Adam and Eve on the earth, they were designed to discover the treasures in creation and develop them while discovering the mysteries in God and enjoying him. Jesus has reconciled us to God the Father so that we can get on with that purpose. In creation and through revelation, we can know God. This is the essence of life eternal.

14. Sell and Give

It is not news to us that fear is a major cause of confusion and paralysis in our lives. When the foundations of our safety and security are threatened, we find fear rearing its monstrous head in our thoughts. So it should not surprise us that many today are paralyzed by fear as the economic foundations of our system are in question. People are afraid to spend, to invest, and to give. They are waiting for some solid sign of stability.

How does the Gospel affect this phenomenon? Are we just supposed to focus on going to church on Sunday and to heaven when we die and to ignore the culture in which we live? Actually, the Gospel addresses this fear head-on. When God gave us eternal life, we became sons of the Father. As sons, we no longer think like orphans. Our Father's provisions are committed to our success in fulfilling the mission he gave us. We aren't victims of the forces of earthly kingdoms. We live under a rule that transcends all other forms of government.

When Jesus came to earth he chose twelve men to whom he would show the workings of the kingdom of God. They witnessed a radical confrontation. When he addressed the human tendency to be anxious, he pointed out that the Father-king cared for even the animal kingdom and the plant kingdom. His point was that if the impersonal kingdoms were so supplied, the sons of the Father would be looked after with even more care and attention. "Of how much more value are you than the birds!" he said (Luke 12:24). Then he gives the clinching conclusion:

*Fear not, little flock, for it is your Father's good pleasure
to give you the kingdom. Sell your possessions and give
to the needy. Provide yourselves with moneybags that do
not grow old, with a treasure in the heavens that does not
fail, where no thief approaches and no moth destroys.
For where your treasure is, there will your heart be also.*

Luke 12:32-34 (ESV)

The Father is a shepherd who assumes the full responsibility
for the condition of his flock. As sheep we are too vulnerable to
take care of ourselves. The Father is one who intensely desires to
give to his children, neither miserly nor lacking in funds. The
Father is a king who intends to give his inheritance to his sons.
With all this in mind then, the sons can mock our obsession with
collecting material wealth by selling and giving to the needy.

This kind of living – sons acting like their Father – would
surely be different from that of the rest of society. He is the
ultimate giver and has held nothing back in his desire to meet the
needs of lost and self-bound orphans. When sons of God sell and
give they are expressing the nature of the kingdom that Jesus
brought to earth. They become the wisest investors in the world
when they realize the only investment guaranteed for eternity is
the gift that costs us something.

This seems almost ridiculous. Surely this is not what Christianity is really about. It sounds strange even to the ears of Christians. It brings to mind the story of the wealthy young man who
came to Jesus asking how he might inherit eternal life (Mark
10:17-31). When Jesus finally told him to sell his possessions and
give to the needy, the man went away sad. Then Jesus remarked
how difficult it is for rich people to enter the kingdom of God.
The disciples were aghast at his words.

Why were they so surprised? The answer is key to understanding the true nature of the Gospel. This young man had all the evidence of righteousness as defined by the Jewish understanding of the Old Testament and the teachings of the Rabbis. Not understanding that the Old Testament was portraying shadows of the coming substance, they had concluded that material wealth was a sign of blessings that were the result of obedience. After all, God had given the elementary principles of creation where being good was rewarded and being bad was punished. He had reinforced this with the covenant made through Moses. "If you keep the covenant, you will be the head and not the tail. You will be the lender and not the borrower, etc." David, the good king, had been wealthy beyond measure and so had his son, Solomon, who built the majestic temple that shouted to the surrounding nations: "There are benefits to knowing our God."

But these were shadows of the real kingdom that would come through Jesus. He would open the way to know God as he knows him. He would be the temple himself. The wealth of access to God as Father would make the riches of Solomon look like a child's piggy bank. A few other rulers were impressed with Solomon's wealth and works, but the Father had given Jesus all the nations as his inheritance.

> ...The Lord said to me, "You are my son; today I have begotten you. Ask of me and I will make the nations your heritage, and the ends of the earth your possession."
> Psalms 2:7-8 (ESV)

The kingdom Jesus introduced to the earth was not about material wealth. Though he never negated the elementary principles of creation, he offered a life that far superseded them. In Jesus' perspective the poor were not products of disobedience, nor were the wealthy beneficiaries of hard work or obedient living. The issue for his kingdom is relating to the Father as sons who manage his resources for his purposes. Real sons care for the nations that Jesus inherited and are investing in claiming them for his glory. They know that the Gospel is the way for mankind to know God as Father. Only a Son can make the introduction, and they are committed to getting the message out.

Sadly, today we more closely identify with the perspective of the rich young man than with Jesus. He obviously felt that he was doing pretty well. He carried the marks of a righteous man: He was rich (evidence that he was obeying the covenant); he was young (evidence that he made progress quickly); and he was cocksure that his qualifications were impeccable. Notice that he wanted to know what he could DO. So Jesus gave him the specific laws designed to show that we couldn't DO enough to inherit eternal life. The young man thought he had qualified, so Jesus exposed his deception. The idol had to be addressed: "Sell and give." If the boy really had walked in the revelation of God, he could do this. The disciples had been called on to make this kind of commitment. They had made the transition, or at least they were making it.

Today, when we read the Bible as a comprehensive instruction book and not as the narrative of God's progressive revelation, we too will confuse the nature of the kingdom of God. We will become guilty of adopting a "prosperity gospel" even though we are embarrassed by the overt shamelessness of TV ministries promising material blessings to those sending in money. When we imply that God's purpose is to display the superiority of his kingdom by the amount of wealth we consume on ourselves, we are promoting a false gospel. When churches boast about the size of their facilities designed to meet the demands of the American consumer compared to the relatively small investments in the true need around the world, we mirror the fascination we have with the opulence of a couple who spend twenty million to build a huge house that only two people occupy. We call that success!

The New Testament doesn't guarantee material success on the basis of obeying biblical principles or based solely on hard work. The New Testament is the substance of the physical and natural shadows of the Old Testament, and features a life of joy and stewardship. Success is measured more by what is given than what is accumulated. The substance is not about building edifices where God can meet with mankind. it is about God building people who live only for the glory of God and will take his word to the nations.

The "prosperity light" gospel has other negative ramifications. With the rate of unemployment higher, many hard-working men and women are struggling with a lack of basics for existence. They have been as obedient as others and have worked diligently, yet they are not being "blessed" according to the expectations of their theology. What did they do wrong? Do the prosperity promises only work for some? And what about those who are not even trying to obey God's laws and are still flourishing? We know that in the end all that will be settled, but what about now?

In the story of the rich young man, it is very interesting that it says that Jesus loved him and said, "One thing you lack. Sell and give." I'm sure that command didn't sound like love to the young man. It sounded crazy and costly. It was an impossible command, given that his trust was in his possessions. Jesus loved him so much he wanted to free him from the false security of works-righteousness and material wealth.

He loves us too much to leave us with the gods of lesser delights when we could know the liberty of living in his wealth.

Some have mentioned that Jesus didn't tell everyone to sell everything and give to the needy, just this man. David Platt remarks that anyone who would take comfort in that is exactly the kind of person Jesus would address with such a command. We desperately want to hold to the shadows and also get the benefits of the substance.

The New Testament Gospel is not about improvement. It is about the impossible. Only by knowing the unspeakable joy of sonship will any of us be willing to abandon the offers of earthly security. The good news is that a new era has dawned, bigger and better than the one that foreshadowed it. The cross shouts the Gospel of hope. Death cannot thwart the purpose of God. He will take the blindness of people, the hatred of hell, and the laws of the universe and make them servants of his glory. The life that Jesus grants is a different kind of life. It is about freedom to live and give for the glory of God. Sons look and act like the Father that begat them.

Conclusion

God has always existed as Father, Son and Holy Spirit. When he created man in his image, he put the relationship of father and son relating by the spirit into physical form. Adam, as male and female, knew God as Father and partnered with him in managing the earth according to his purpose. God has always delighted in his Son, and so delighted in Adam as his son on earth.

The intrusion of sin into this relationship introduced an orphan mentality to the earth. The one created to delight in the Father was afraid of him. However, God's purpose of revealing the majesty of his grace would be fulfilled in the coming of Jesus as the last Adam who would demonstrate for all in heaven and on earth the glory of a man living as a son on earth.

This has happened! Now we are invited into that father-son relationship because Jesus crucified the orphan-life on the cross and the Holy Spirit has come to regenerate us and lead us into the full joy of that relationship. It is foolish for us to continue living like orphans when all things are ready for us to embrace our inheritance and get about the original mandate of partnering with our Father in managing his creation. There are untold mysteries to unlock and unfathomable treasures to be found.

We cannot afford to live under condemnation that has been canceled. Nor can we excuse our plight on the basis of our disqualification. We are called to change the way we perceive reality and thus rise above the meager human goal of survival or self-improvement. We have been given the Spirit who demonstrated his power by raising Jesus from the dead. We can confidently live for the glory of our Father, praising the Son and following the lead of the Holy Spirit. God's sons on earth are reconciled and ready to get about doing what God designed us to do. **We are orphans no more!**

Acknowledgements

Without Wade Trimmer, this book probably would not have happened. Wade put some of these messages together on his own and "without permission" and demonstrated what could be done. He provided a generous dose of encouragement as well as some technical advice on publishing. Thanks Wade!

Tom Hall provided compilation and editing support. David Hall put the book together and walked it through the publishing process. Karis Hall provided a great deal of administrative help and support. Thanks to the Hall family for all their work and support in making this book a reality.

I would especially like to thank all of the subscribers to Dudley's Monthly Message. Through the years you have been an inspiration, a point of accountability and a wonderful audience to whom to preach the messages God has placed in my heart. I consider you family You've heard these messages before; I hope you are blessed and God speaks to you as sons as you read them here.

About the Author

Dudley Hall is a recognized teacher who has been blessed with extraordinary gifts for equipping the body of Christ. He holds a Masters of Divinity from Southwestern Baptist Theological Seminary and a Bachelors degree from Samford University. Dudley's formal ministry began in college leading youth evangelism crusades. Sensing a need for discipleship training beyond the initial "sinner's prayer" experience, he developed a follow-up program to citywide evangelistic crusades that touched thousands. He has helped plant churches throughout the United States and Africa and was a founder of the Emmaus Road Ministry School.

Dudley is passionate about the centrality of Jesus Christ and the proclamation and practice of the New Testament Gospel. He mentors young men, business leaders, pastors and ministry leaders, connecting the generations in a single-minded pursuit of knowing the Father as only a son can. Dudley is gifted in empowering men to embrace their masculine spirituality and leadership roles. His teaching and discipleship materials are used around the world.

Dudley has authored several books including *Grace Works*, *Incense & Thunder*, *Glad to be Left Behind*, and, *Men In Their Own Skin*. He is a sought-after speaker, an engaging preacher, an effective consultant, and a trusted spiritual father. As the founder and President of Successful Christian Living Ministries (SCLM), Dudley is most at home on the beautiful 350 acre Tesoro Escondido Ranch discipling and training leaders in all spheres of life. Dudley and his wife, Betsy, live in Grapevine, Texas. They have two grown children and four grandkids.